Attacked is a riveting story and a heart-wrenching account of one man's journey with gain, loss, heartbreak, grief, restoration, and ultimately, HOPE. I have known Brian now for many years and have watched him up close and from a distance learn to overcome, with God's amazing help, huge hurdles inwardly and outwardly. If you know of anyone who has suffered trauma, loss, heartache and deep grief, Brian's story is for you or for someone you may know. The honest, raw, and real way that Brian has written offers a glimpse into a tragedy that was evil, murderous, violent and debilitating, an event that set in motion a set of circumstances you would not wish on anyone. Brian's willingness to forgive and ultimately come into an intimate relationship with Father God is telling and triumphant. The statement from scripture has proven true: "God works all things together for good to them who love God and are called according to His purpose." This is truly a story of God doing this in and for and through Brian's life, especially where one night, it all changed.

— David Dishroon
Senior Pastor, Changepoint, Tauranga, NZ

I have known Brian for years. I sit by him in church and we get in trouble for laughing too much. Joy and peace are always around him, and I find him an endearing character. The importance of Brian sharing his story is immense. He is a quiet and humble man, the quintessential Kiwi guy, who fell victim to violence and walked through extreme trauma. I hold him in high regard as a friend who I can trust. His strong faith will impress you and encourage you.

— Mark Richard 'Bull' Allen
NZ Rugby Union Player and TV Personality
Former All Black (1993)

I was overwhelmed with emotions as my friend, Brian, told me the story of his life. As he revealed his past, I thought to myself, *What would I be like if all of that happened to me? Would I be able to forgive?* Brian's surrender to God's perspective on evil was very encouraging. He is a walking testimony to the power of God in a believer's life and his story needs to be told! This book will help so many of us who can be sorely affected by the actions of others. Brian's story is a triumph of God's grace and mercy in a fallen world. You, too, will see there are no 'victims' in God's kingdom.

— **Philip Pigneri**
C3 City Church, Tauranga

Attacked is a vulnerable and moving account of incredible loss. The author takes us on an intensely personal journey through traumatic events and the fallout after. It's a Job-like story of the bottom being pulled out from under a person's hard-fought world and the ensuing struggles with faith, pain and hopelessness. It's ultimately a story, however, of the healing power of radical forgiveness, that no one is meant to make it on their own, and that there is hope of a return to joy no matter how deep the darkness. As a counsellor, I especially appreciated that this story is written by a man. We need accounts like this from a male perspective of mental health to encourage other men to seek help sooner.

— **Heather Pound**
Counsellor and Author of *Known*

ATTACKED

TORN CURTAIN PUBLISHING
Auckland, New Zealand
www.torncurtainpublishing.com

ISBN Softcover 978-1-991299-69-7
ISBN ePub 978-1-991299-70-3

All details included in this book are written from the author's best recollection and perspective. Some names and identifying details of people described in this book have been altered to protect their privacy.

This book contains a graphic account of the author's personal experience, including physical assault.

Unless otherwise noted, all scripture references are from the New International Version®, NIV®. Copyright © 1973, 1978, 1984, 2011 by Biblica, Inc.™ Used by permission of Zondervan. All rights reserved worldwide.

Typeset in RC Rocket, Ralway and Minion

Cataloging in Publishing Data
  Title: Attacked: A real-life story of a violent home invasion and the unravelling of an ordinary New Zealand family
  Author: Brian Wilkinson
  Subjects: Forgiveness, reconciliation, family breakdown, marriage, mental health, Christian living, pastoral resource, gun violence, community issues.

A copy of this title is held at the National Library of New Zealand.

ATTACKED

A REAL-LIFE STORY OF A
VIOLENT HOME INVASION

and the unravelling of an ordinary New Zealand family

Brian Wilkinson

Attack on family

NZPA

Hamilton

A 23-year-old man who held a family hostage and threatened to kill the father has been sentenced to six and a half years' jail.

The February incident at Te Kowhai, near Hamilton, was recounted in the High Court at Hamilton at the sentencing of ████████████████, who appeared before Justice Hammond.

████████, unemployed, pleaded guilty to five charges of kidnapping and one each of aggravated wounding, aggravated breaking and entering and unlawfully taking a motor vehicle.

Justice Hammond said on Thursday that ████████ forced his way into the family home, attacked Mr Brian Wilkinson with the butt of a rifle and threatened to kill him.

Mr Wilkinson's family, including his three young children, were awoken and watched as ████████ tied him up, held a gun to his head and repeated his threats.

He told the family he had held a grudge against Mr Wilkinson for some time.

Justice Hammond said the family members had then escaped from the house, and ████████ responded by running around the property screaming abuse and saying he would kill them all if he found them.

Justice Hammond said drugs and alcohol seemed to have been at the root of ████████ offending.

CONTENTS

PROLOGUE

BRILLIANT RACE! I THOUGHT, STRETCHING MY ARMS ABOVE MY HEAD as I stood up from the couch and headed towards the open door leading onto our front deck. *Well worth staying up to see our boys take the Cup.* I looked at the clock. Half-past midnight. Sue and the kids had gone to bed a few hours earlier, and the rest of the house was already locked up for the night.

I'd stayed up late watching our national team race in one of the finals of the America's Cup. New Zealand has a strong sailing heritage, but the famous New York Yacht Club had held the Cup for over a hundred years until Australia finally managed to wrestle it away to the Southern Hemisphere. New Zealand entered the game three years later, won the Cup, but lost by protest. By 1995, with local sailing legend Peter Blake managing the team, it looked like we were in a great position to bring home the Cup for the first time. Few countries were able to muster the physical and technical boatbuilding and sailing skills needed to compete in the elite America's Cup, and I was hooked on the sport.

It was also a pretty big deal for our country. Although we're great sailors and are used to punching above our weight, we are a small economy, and the America's Cup team that year needed an innovative way of funding the campaign. When Peter Blake put out the call to all Kiwis, "Get yer socks on!" the whole country rallied to the

1

challenge. People up and down the country bought a pair of Team New Zealand red socks, and for weeks, people could be seen wearing them in anticipation. *Of course we would win!* Which was why that evening, I was sitting watching television in my boxers and red socks with a nice cold drink beside me.

What a finale. Looking out, I could barely make out the little path that led through the trees to the fruit and veggie stall at the front of our driveway. The summer air was balmy at this time of night, and the moonlit shadows danced across the lawn as I reached to pull the curtains and close the door when . . . *wham!*

My head exploded with searing pain.

"I'm gonna kill you, man!"

I recognised that voice.

As I collapsed to the floor, my entire world collapsed with me.

1
CONFIDENT AND CAREFREE

IN MANY WAYS, WE WERE A NORMAL FAMILY. A FOUR-GENERATION farming family with deep roots in the South, an incredibly picturesque part of New Zealand with white sandy beaches, beautiful rivers, and acres of native forest.

My grandparents on both sides were what everybody called 'the salt of the earth'. Their ancestors had said goodbye to 'Old England', accepting the offer of free passage to the far-away colony of New Zealand, where the new governing body had promised freehold land to farmers in an attempt to kickstart the fledgling economy. Like so many new settlers, they arrived with only their faith, farming knowledge, some tools, seeds, and a couple of breeding sheep. In every other respect, they were starting from scratch.

The land my family was given couldn't have been more idyllic. Long, hot summer days and a snowfall or two during the winter made our valley in the South Island of New Zealand a wonderful place for my great-great-great-grandparents to begin their new lives. Over time, the farms were passed down from one generation to the next until, by the time I was born, four generations of my father's family had grown up, married, and raised children on farms of their own.

With great-grandparents, grandparents, aunts, uncles and cousins all living nearby, my days were filled with riding my bike, swimming in the nearby stony-bottom river, or dropping in to help separate the cream from the cow's milk or watch my grandad work on his home-built helicopter and enjoy my nana's fresh baking. Then I'd go home to our farm where I'd be driving tractors, helping Mum and Dad in the vegetable garden, or mustering the sheep with Dad.

My father was a leader in the local church—a church my forebears had helped establish when they arrived in the region. I loved Sundays—especially Sunday School, where my nana on my mother's side taught the most lovely bible lessons. *God loves you. God knew you before you were born. God knows your name. God has a wonderful plan for your life.* I entered my teenage years with complete confidence that whatever happened in life, all would be well.

But not everything was well. Dad was a commanding figure, much like his father. He worked hard on the farm growing grain, tobacco and potatoes, but it was a constant struggle and Dad was never fully content. He had never wanted to be a farmer, but he had little choice. The fun he had with us as little children became a distant memory as we entered our teenage years. I loved my family and held great respect for my dad and mum, who did their best to provide for us all. My siblings and I would often get into mischief and received periodic spankings to keep us in line.

My greatest solace was sport. Every day at the start of the rugby season, my best friend and I would run and park ourselves with great anticipation on the school veranda in case we could overhear the coach discussing the teams. We were mainly concerned with who the captains were going to be. Finally, the announcement came during school assembly one morning: "Brian Wilkinson, Captain of the rugby team." At that point, nothing else mattered. I was captain of my cricket team as well.

I'm not sure exactly what made Dad decide that we should sell up and move. Perhaps it was because our farm was quite small, and without the acreage to grow a profitable crop like tobacco, the income was down, along with the wool prices. Dad had a difficult relationship with his father. Maybe he'd had enough. Maybe he wanted to prove that he could make it on his own. Whatever the reason, our holidays now included scouring the whole country, North and South Islands, for a suitable farm.

My life was thoroughly taken up with rugby when Dad decided to buy a farm just north of Auckland in an area called Dairy Flat. Moving to the 'big smoke' was a great upheaval for our family, and I struggled to adjust to my new life. Mostly, I missed my grandparents. I was also a country boy in a big city school, and I was bullied for being 'different'.

Dad, however, thrived on the challenge. With a hundred and twenty cows, our farm was known as a 'town supply' farm, which meant we supplied part of the urban demand for milk by calving and milking year-round. The best part of helping on the farm for me was driving a tractor. Farming in the North Island was not as easy as it had been in the South. The heavy clay soil became very wet in the winter and as dry as concrete in the summer, but it gave my father the chance to try some of his entrepreneurial ideas—breeding Friesian cows (which were popular for their high-volume milk production) and using some of our land to grow watermelons and boysenberries (which seemed to do fine in our clay soil). In time, Dad saw a development opportunity and bought an uncleared block of land forty-five minutes north of Auckland in Puhoi. We would go together to cut the gorse and tea tree and bring it into the pasture for the beef cattle.

Church youth group became an anchor for me over this time, and when I passed my driver's licence test at the age of fifteen, life couldn't have been better. As a youth group, we'd get together for all kinds of activities—games nights, car rallies, barbeques . . . even going to stock car racing in the local area. I felt a sense of freedom which made me incredibly happy. I was making my way in our new environment with like-minded friends at my side. We had so much fun that I was never attracted to bars or nightclubs and never became involved with alcohol or drugs. At the same time, God was becoming very real to me—not just someone 'up in the sky' as I'd imagined him when I was a child.

When Billy Graham, the famous American evangelist, came to New Zealand, Dad took our whole family to hear him preach. That night, as we stood right at the back of the stadium and listened, the tug on my heart was palpable. In that moment, I felt so close to God, so safe, loved and secure. When Billy Graham invited people to 'give their lives to Jesus,' I was ready to say yes. It was a very sweet moment in my life. Like every teenager, I'd had my ups and downs, but life was full of promise and hope, I had wonderful friends, and nothing much bothered me. Little did I know what lay ahead.

2
WAIKATO FARMER

A T THE AGE OF SEVENTEEN, I WAS CONSIDERING MY CAREER PATH. *Maybe I could be an electrician,* I thought. After all, I enjoyed solving electrical problems and working with farm machinery. *Or maybe I could train as a pilot.* I'd always been intrigued with flight—ever since I'd watched my grandfather hand-riveting metal plates together to create the body of his remarkable 'helicopter'. I loved seeing him pull together all sorts of recycled parts, new levers and dials, and simply thousands of rivets. In my ten-year-old imagination, I could see myself climbing into the pilot's seat with Grandad, rising up into the air with the big rotor spinning and looking down on all the sheep and cows and people on their farms. Maybe we'd fly over the town and my school.

On the final day of construction, Grandad fitted the engine. The two-seater helicopter looked marvellous. It was the test flight, so I wasn't allowed to climb in—next time, maybe. Grandad told me to stand at a safe distance. The rotor started to turn with a loud, promising whir, and I put my hands over my ears. Up it lifted slightly, up a bit more, and still further until it was completely off the ground . . . then with an uncertain tilt to the left, a sudden drop and a dangerous judder, the spinning rotor caught a fence post and the whole thing flipped and fell, never to fly again! Grandad wasn't hurt, but he was mightily disappointed after all the hours of work he'd put in. The helicopter was dragged back to the shed, abandoned as a broken dream for as long as I could remember. But like my grandfather, I wasn't easily dissuaded. *Maybe this was my opportunity. Maybe I could learn to fly?*

◆ ◆ ◆

Then an unexpected decision by Dad thrust me towards a new possibility.

Dad sold our two farms near Auckland and, with his substantial capital gain, bought a farm in the Waikato region near a pleasant, rural town called Morrinsville. The Waikato is a very fertile, highly productive area of New Zealand and many farmers dream of owning land there. Our new farm was beautifully presented, with fields of barley and perfect land for grazing beef cattle. The home was spacious, elegant, and much nicer than anything we'd been used to. For the first time in my life, my three brothers and I didn't have to share the same room.

The moment we settled in the Waikato region, I made my decision: farming would be my career.

◆ ◆ ◆

Farming in the Waikato was unlike anything I'd experienced before. For one thing, the fields were divided by tall, unruly barberry hedges rather than fences. Hedges like these busily crisscrossed the fertile pastureland of this region, making it look well-managed and prosperous. But these towering hedges served a more important purpose: they kept the cattle from straying out onto the roads and provided an effective windbreak that sheltered the crops. The only problem was that the hedges needed to be regularly cut back into neat lines ... which usually required the services of a contractor with a huge, oversized hedge-cutting machine.

I had been helping out on a neighbour's farm with chores and milking until one day the neighbour announced: "I've got a contractor coming to cut the hedges. Can you come over and help?" Sure enough, when I turned up, there was the tractor, with a movable boom out to one side and two huge, circular blades hanging above it like a giant skill saw. After the usual greetings, the driver set the machine into position and began to angle the blades. When everything looked ready to go, our neighbour asked me to come with him. "I need to get started on another job," he told me. "Can you stay here with the contractor in case he needs anything?" I gave a quick nod. *Sure thing.*

Eventually, the contractor powered up the motor. I was surprised when a shrill, almost unbearable, whine came from the fast-spinning blades. *Never heard that before,* I thought to myself, backing away to watch from a safe distance. The driver of the tractor acknowledged my move with a nod of his head. Soon, I was mesmerised as I watched the sharp blades bite easily into the thick woody hedge, reshaping it into an impressive vertical wall with a precisely flattened top.

Spring was coming in full force, and I knew the spikey, barberry hedges would thicken up quickly and be as good as any wire fence at keeping the cows in. It was just as well the hedges were kept compact and formed tall, impenetrable walls, because the cows were constantly in search of any 'grass that was greener'. I don't know how many animals I'd herded back into their paddocks during my life growing up on our farms. *Better to keep them in properly in the first place,* I mused, when ... *Bang!* Suddenly, I was hurled to the ground.

The driver of the tractor saw me fall, slammed his machine to an instant stop, and began yelling as he raced over to where I lay, seemingly unconscious. One look told him the story: a piece of barbed wire had wrapped itself around my face, slashing my cheek from mouth to ear, and I was bleeding freely.

I regained consciousness while the two men were carrying me to the farmhouse. "You'll be right mate," the driver smiled, "Not too much blood lost!" The look on the face of the farmer's wife told a different story. Wrapping my face and neck in a towel, they rushed me to the medical centre. "The barbed wire must have been hurled out of the hedge at speed by one of the rotating saw blades!" I heard the doctor say as he began stitching the inside of my mouth. By the end of the day, I had thirty-five stitches from mouth to left ear, but I was alive. I couldn't help wondering how, in such a large paddock, that single piece of barbed wire had found its mark. *It's a miracle I wasn't decapitated. God must have his eye on me,* I concluded. I had survived a brush with death—and I had a scar that would forever memorialise the start of my new career.

Perhaps the accident impacted our family in ways I wasn't aware of at the time. All I know is that in the following months, my parents' relationship spiralled downwards. Dad had probably been considering it silently for a while, but when he told us he was moving to Australia alone, I thought, *Really? Alone?* It felt terribly abrupt.

My thoughts tumbled in angry chaos. Dad had been my hero, a man with high integrity and strong morals. *Now he was going to leave us? What did he think he was doing?* From my teenage perspective, this was the most selfish and destructive thing my dad could have done. *He's abandoning me ... and my brothers and sister. He's leaving Mum to deal with all these problems on her own.* I couldn't reconcile it all in my mind.

In the meantime, Mum was doing all she could to look after the family, but she too was struggling with the fallout. I did my best to help her manage the farm but eventually, she sold it and moved back to Auckland, taking my younger brother and sister with her.

For the first time in my life, I was on my own. Though I often felt homesick, I learned to pick myself up and positively look ahead. I had studies to complete as well as practical work as part of my farming diploma. I still enjoyed going to church, there was plenty of good camaraderie, and most of all, I had my mates. Summer was coming, and that meant Saturday nights at the stock car track with our girlfriends, watching the drivers hurl their V8s around the track and then hanging around to hear stories from the drivers afterwards. The speed, the fumes, the sound, the power, the fun ... my life was bliss.

3
SHOCKED AND SURPRISED

A FEW MONTHS LATER, I TOOK UP A JOB SHARE-MILKING FOR A local dairy farmer. An old farmhouse was provided for me, and for the first time in my life, I was living alone. The house itself had what some might call character. It was built on very dodgy, sloping piles. If I placed an egg on the kitchen bench, it would roll slowly but predictably towards the south.

As a busy bachelor working from dawn to dusk, I soon decided I needed help with the cooking, the housework and the garden. I advertised the job in exchange for free food and lodging, and sure enough, I received several replies the same week. This was my first time interviewing potential workers, and when an older couple turned up, I offered them the job. It seemed like the perfect arrangement for both of us.

At first, things seemed to be working out very well. John and Sheila made my daily life a lot easier, and I was glad to be back to eating regular meals instead of opening a couple of cans of baked beans for lunch every day. But it wasn't to last. After work one evening, when I walked into the kitchen to greet my new housekeeper as usual, she turned to see me and began to shriek. *What was going on?!* There was no time to figure it out. Suddenly, a glass flew through the air and hit me on the side of my face, then another. *Crikey,* I thought, *I'm in trouble here!* By now, Sheila had moved to the doorway. There was a strange look in her eyes. I knew I needed to get out—and fast. Without another thought, I launched myself out through the kitchen window, smashing the glass as I went.

I discovered later on that Sheila had been diagnosed with a mental health disorder, which she had evidently been battling for a long time. Eventually, she was admitted to a facility where she could receive treatment, leaving her husband on his own with me. *We'll make it work,* I thought, ever the optimist.

But John had his own set of problems. One evening, I spotted him reeling and staggering an unsteady path back home and clutching a brown paper bag. "What on earth are you doing?" I called out. I was completely naïve about his activities and hadn't guessed what was happening. It wasn't until after I'd helped him out of a couple of his mishaps that I came to understand he had a big problem with alcohol. More than once, he took his car into town and drove headlong into a drainage ditch along the side of the road on his way home.

"Err Brian, I've just driven past Ol' John. You'd better get the tractor out, mate. He's put himself in the ditch again!" a neighbour phoned in amusement.

"Yup, better go and retrieve him." I jumped into the tractor and found John's car in a ditch not far from the farm. There he was, still in the driver's seat, fast asleep. A gentle, unconcerned snore escaped his lips as I bent over to help him out.

I'd never had much experience with drunks before this, but I soon learned the ropes. Take him home, give him a good sleep and some coffee, or drop him into a cold bath to try and sober him up. Perhaps John was his own worst enemy, but he was a lovely guy who'd do anything for anyone and, having caught a glimpse of the situation he'd been living with for many years, I felt genuine compassion for him.

◆ ◆ ◆

Over time, John moved on, and I was back to living alone in the big old farmhouse. Thankfully, I had started to connect with some great new friends at a large church in Hamilton. This wasn't at all like the churches I'd been to before. No organ, no hymns, no quiet sermons where the farmers struggled to stay awake. In this church, the worship was led by a full band, and the pastor preached interesting sermons about real-life issues. To a born and bred country boy it all felt very sophisticated, and for a few weeks I felt a bit out of place. But none of that mattered when I spotted the girl playing the piano and my heart missed a beat. How could I ever get to know a talented, gorgeous city girl like her? *Ah well, dreams are free!* I reasoned to myself and tried to put her out of my mind. Thankfully, there were plenty of opportunities to socialise. The mothers of the church quickly decided I was sweet and would be a good match for their daughters, so most weekends I could rely on an invitation to dinner at someone's house. I really enjoyed weekends, when I'd head into town with other young adults from the church to catch a movie, have coffee, or enjoy the stock car racing.

◆ ◆ ◆

One warm summer evening, after watching the stock car racing, we returned to the home of one of the church families for a late evening snack. This was the 'done thing' on Saturday evenings after stock cars. It was quite late when we arrived, and most of the family was in bed. Quietly, we opened the door and walked into the house ... and I almost fell over my own feet when I saw whose home it was. Waiting up to welcome us was the beautiful girl on the piano! "Hi! I'm Sue," she introduced herself. I mumbled a few awkward words to her as she served up hot drinks and huge slices of homemade cake. I was both gobsmacked and smitten.

It took me three weeks to pluck up the courage to ask Sue out on a date. "Yes!" she said, and that date quickly led to another ... and another. We both doubled up in laughter when Sue told me that she'd been eyeing me at church too and had deliberately waited until that evening after the stock car racing to meet me. Our friendship quickly grew and soon we were inseparable. Sue loved the farm and visited me as often as she could between her studies at the teachers' training college. She was bright and bubbly, and she loved to learn anything and everything about my life on the farm. For my part, I was as happy as a pig in mud.

Three months later, we were engaged. Sue was nineteen, I was twenty-two, and our excitement was impossible to contain. In just six months, we would be married! Quickly, the plans began swinging into place. My Dutch father-in-law coughed and spluttered at the cost of our very modest reception, but later we laughed about it together. There was something warm and winsome about Sue's family culture, and I felt genuinely welcomed in. Sue's parents and siblings really enjoyed debating among themselves, which to me sounded boisterous and opinionated until I realised the depth of respect that bound them all together. In this very loving family, I felt accepted in a way I hadn't known in my growing-up years.

On our wedding day, we were surrounded by friends and family, and as we waved goodbye for our honeymoon, I knew our livelihoods were in good hands—my new mother-in-law and some of her friends had offered to milk all our cows twice a day while we went caravanning around the South Island for a whole month! What a feeling to receive such gracious help and support as we set out together. The kindness of our friends and family at that time has stayed with me ever since.

When we returned to the farm, we felt in every sense that we were coming home. I continued farming, while Sue finished her teacher training and gave piano lessons to neighbouring children. On Friday nights, we headed to church together, where we ran a kids' club for the local children. It soon grew, until we had quite a crowd of kids surrounding us! This was our community, and we felt very content to be giving something worthwhile to local children.

4

SECOND CHANCES

AFTER FOUR YEARS OF MARRIAGE, WE BECAME A FAMILY OF THREE. What pure delight it was to celebrate the arrival of our firstborn son, Jason—and on my birthday! Sue had suffered a miscarriage before falling pregnant with Jason, and our family had prayed faithfully for his safe delivery ever since they heard he was on his way. What an easy-going, calm personality he had! We were very proud. Two years later, we welcomed our first daughter, Michelle, and two years after her, our second beautiful daughter, Sarah, arrived. I felt God had blessed us beyond measure with these little ones, who were now our responsibility! I often wondered with a sense of quiet excitement about God's plan for our future. Our children were our joy and delight.

In our early years of married life, Sue and I had moved around the Waikato region share-farming. In my early twenties, I didn't understand much about building equity, but we had managed to save enough deposit to purchase a property of our own. With our little family complete, we decided to turn our hand to something new, and with the deposit we had saved, bought a large, export apple-growing orchard very close to Hamilton. We were full of ambition.

Our share-milking days were behind us. The export industry was thriving. There was no limit to what lay ahead!

What we didn't know was that New Zealand was on the brink of a major economic shift. Almost as soon as we took ownership of the orchard, a set of economic reforms known as *Rogernomics*—named after the then minister of finance—was introduced. This became a defining moment for the New Zealand primary industries sector. Financial subsidies were abruptly removed, and overnight, farmers found themselves without government protection.

Before Sue and I had even begun paying it off, our mortgage interest rate rose to a huge twenty-two percent. Farmers were going broke all around us, with some even committing suicide. It was a financially devastating time for the rural community and a massive blow to us, having just purchased our business.

The bank was supportive, but soon we were borrowing just to pay the interest on our mortgage. We were going backwards fast. Being the 'she'll be right' kind of guy that I was, I didn't comprehend the depth of what was happening. If only I could have turned to my dad. With his natural acumen for business, his advice would have been invaluable to me. Instead, he was now living in Australia and a long way out of my life.

Before long, Sue and I faced the looming loss of our property and all our savings. *What's the answer, Lord?!* I questioned. My way of dealing with big decisions was to bowl on in and expect God to look after us—and in his grace, he did. In the weeks ahead, John, a lovely friend who had been very successful in the farming industry, offered to invest in our business. Gratefully, we accepted. Sue had grown up with his daughters, and John thought the world of her. He wanted to see us succeed in the business for our benefit. "I'm not in it for the profit," he said. "I just want to see you get back on your feet."

With a simple verbal agreement in place, John became our business mentor and investor. After buying the land outright, we leased it back to the business. When the dairy farm next door came onto the market, John put up the finance and we purchased that property as well. We would subdivide the land, sell off the half that had a house and cowshed, and develop the balance of the land.

Well, that wasn't too hard, I told myself. The new property soon became highly productive. Within a couple of years we were employing a significant number of workers. Exports were going well. Our presence in the community was appreciated. By God's grace, we were back in business.

In truth, though I didn't know it then, I was starting to imagine there was an invincibility about me and my business dealings. I decided it was time to build our own packing sheds.

Building our own fruit packing shed rather than outsourcing the packing was a groundbreaking step for the business, and it took our capacity to a new level. Before long, I was elected president of the Waikato Fruit Growers Association and Sue became the secretary. Expansion happened quickly from that point. We bought more land, purchased freight trucks, and soon began packing apples for other orchardists in the area. With the increased need for staff, we began employing a large number of transient packers, as well as a permanent core of locals. Sam was my right-hand man at the time, helping me manage our workforce of fifty during the height of the season.

But with the transient workforce came a problem I really didn't know how to handle. Drugs were a constant feature among our transient workers, and being naïve on that subject, I found myself having to cope with the fallout as one worker after another would turn up unfit for work after a night of excessive use. Having received so much kindness myself, I was also keen to give others a second chance. We were often approached by guys who, because of past convictions, had trouble finding a job. I was glad to be able to offer them basic seasonal work, picking fruit, driving forklifts, or assembling cardboard boxes for packing the fruit. This worked well at first. The business had a steady supply of workers, and guys who needed to get back into the workforce had the opportunity.

But some of the guys let drugs get the better of them. One day, Sam came to me. "I have a friend who could do with some hours," he said. I was more than happy to trust Sam's judgment. "Put him on," I replied. Working in the fresh air and earning a regular income was all it took for some guys to come clean. But it soon became apparent that Sam's friend wasn't up to scratch. After a number of complaints, I knew we had to let him go.

"This is not working," I said to the young guy standing in front of me one day. "I'm really sorry to do this, but we'll need to let you go." I disliked this part of the job the most. *Everyone deserves another chance,* my mind told me. But the team wasn't happy. This guy had been with us for two months and he was still coming to work stoned. He had to go.

I wasn't prepared for the fallout. "You can't fire me for this!" yelled the worker, but I stood my ground. "I'm sorry, mate. It's over."

Tensions were high as I walked back to the office. The guy I had just fired followed me. "You can't do this," he insisted. "I've done nothing wrong!"

"When I employed you, part of the agreement was no drugs or alcohol at work."

The young guy grabbed my collar and held me against the wall. "You haven't heard the end of this, Brian!" he snarled at me as he stormed out of the office.

Was that a threat? I wondered, but I kept the thought to myself. *Generally, we have a wonderful work environment. We're always laughing, and our productivity is good. Things should be fine.* I sent the drugged-up young man on his way and didn't give the incident much thought. It was a busy time of year, and the business needed my focus.

Looking around at the life we had built, I felt a sense of satisfaction. Our children were growing up in much the same environment that I had enjoyed as a child. Most of their life was spent outdoors, frolicking on the lawn with our two dogs, riding their bikes or go-karts, and picking fruit or lending a hand in the packhouse whenever they wanted. We worked from daylight until dark, much like my parents and grandparents, but we enjoyed the simple things of life. As well as exporting apples, we took on a fresh fruit and vegetable shop, which we developed into a trendy produce stall just along the road from our home. Jason, Michelle and Sarah worked alongside us, planting strawberries and harvesting an abundant crop of pears, peaches and vegetables to sell to our local community.

And just like in the South Island valley of my childhood, we had our wonderful extended family nearby. Every week, Sue's dad would pop out to visit, bringing his crossword and sitting down in the orchard where he'd enjoy a cup of tea and help out wherever he could. Whenever Sue and I had fruit growers' functions to attend, or events at church, we could rely on her parents to come over and look after the kids.

Sue's sister became a sister to me as well, and her brothers and their families were our closest friends. Often on a Friday night, we'd all head over to Sue's parents' house for a round of cards. *Klaverjas*—the Dutch card game—is a more complicated version of Five Hundred, but adults and children all joined in together with gusto. At the end of the night, we'd say our goodbyes, drive the short distance back to our rural home, and tuck the children into their beds.

Our home was a warm, safe haven for the family. With business picking back up, Sue and I had set about remodelling our three-bedroom house to accommodate our growing family and to create more entertaining space. Sue often invited friends over to our house and loved hosting special occasions. She was also a keen gardener with an eye for beauty. A hedge of flowering shrubs at the front of our driveway gently curved its way beyond the beautiful flat lawn and garden to the orchard beyond. *I'll never get tired of coming home,* I often thought as I guided a sleepy child up the stairs to the front deck, patted our dogs, and opened the sliding doors.

I remember listening to a man share his story in church one week. Despite God's incredible goodness in his life, I was struck by the extraordinary hardships this man had endured. I leaned over to Sue. "Gosh, our lives have gone pretty well," I whispered. "We're already in our late thirties and we don't have much of a testimony at all!"

Just two weeks later, I had to take back those words.

5
WITHOUT WARNING

THERE WAS NO WARNING WHEN THE BLOW HIT MY FOREHEAD. Falling to the floor, I curled myself into a ball in an attempt to protect myself as a heavy boot slammed repeatedly into my head and chest. *What was happening?* I tried to move, but all I could feel was excruciating pain. Prising my eyes open, I couldn't take in what I was seeing. Blood was everywhere, splattered on the wall, on the ceiling, the curtains, and all over the carpet where I lay. I felt like I was in a movie, just watching this happening to someone else. *Crash!* I tried to blink, but the blood was streaming down my face and into my eyes. All I could make out was a steel spike sticking out the butt end of a modified shotgun. The wooden stock had shattered from the impact with my head.

Why hadn't the dogs barked to warn me of an intruder? Maybe they were fast asleep . . . or maybe they knew it was just Sam. Sam was frequently at our house. If there was a problem in the orchard or the packing sheds, he'd pop over to find me. Sometimes he'd come over to our house after work and stay for a drink or dinner with the family. *What had gone wrong?*

Dropping the gun, Sam ripped the telephone line off the wall. By now, I was in and out of consciousness. Grabbing my arms, Sam yanked them behind my back and began tying my wrists together with the cord of the phone. I tried to gather my thoughts, but I couldn't think clearly. My mind dropped into a blank space of emptiness, trying to make sense of the situation. Then, in a sudden moment of consciousness, I began to panic. *Sue . . . and the kids!* They'd gone to bed hours ago. *Where were they?* I needed to get them out of the house, but I couldn't move. Sam was pacing back and forth in front of me like an angry, manic bear.

"I'm going to kill you, man!" he yelled, slamming his size twelve, steel-toed work boots into me over and over again. *He's loaded with drugs,* I realised. Even in my confusion, I registered the hate in his eyes. I'd seen that look before. This wasn't going to end well.

Suddenly, I heard an exclamation from the hallway. I tried to turn my head, but even before I saw her face, I knew it was Sue. I'd never seen such a terrified look before. A wave of shock and confusion flooded my mind. *Why was he doing this?* My mind went back to the incident in the packing shed office eight months earlier. *Sam's friend? Was that what this was about?*

My mind swirled with emotions. *How had I let this happen to Sue and the kids?* I tried to move my wrists in an attempt to loosen the cord, but it didn't give. "Just leave us alone," I wanted to say, but the words didn't make it out of my mouth. Sam had a sawn-off shotgun and was pointing it at my head. "Bring the kids now!" he shouted at Sue.

I watched Sue move reluctantly down the hallway to the bedrooms. I knew she was trying to stay calm and think about what to do. She walked into the girls' bedroom first. Only one of our daughters was in her bed! Where was our nine-year-old? Seeing the open window,

Sue leaned out to find Michelle hiding outside on the ground. Her mind was in a quandary. What should she do? *There's no telling what Sam will do if his demands aren't met,* she decided. Trembling, she helped Michelle back inside and ushered the girls towards the lounge room.

I cringed when Sam strode into the kitchen, pulled a large knife from the cutlery drawer, and began pacing in front of me once again. The short-barrelled gun seemed to have jammed and his whole body was shaking as he tried to use the knife to free up the mechanism.

By now, Sue had come back into the lounge. Our three children stood beside her in horror. Suddenly, my mind cleared. My ribs felt like they'd been broken, and I knew I wouldn't be able to move very fast. I glanced at the clock on the kitchen wall. 1 a.m. I looked at Sam. "Can I sit up there?" I asked, pointing my head towards the couch. He nodded. I fumbled my way up off the floor and motioned for Jason and Michelle to sit beside me. *At least if we sat close, maybe I could protect them.* Sue was on a nearby chair, holding Sarah, who kept looking at me and whimpering.

By now, Sam was focused on the gun—unloading it, reloading it, swearing and threatening as he pointed it around wildly at us. Petrified, Jason tried to negotiate with him. "Sam, you know us. What do you want? Take anything and just go."

"Shut up or your head's gonna be blown off too," Sam yelled, pointing the firearm at Jason. His voice sounded more agitated than ever. "I'm gonna kill your father."

"Sam," Sue spoke calmly, ". . . you can't do this to the children. You know them, you've helped them with their go-carts, they've helped you pick the apples. You can't shoot their father in front of them." She hoped the familiarity in her voice would help soothe him and bring him to his senses. Sue knew Sam—he'd accepted his paycheck from her every week, and they'd often chatted together. He liked her. They'd laughed and joked together often.

"Okay," Sam finally conceded. "I won't kill him in front of the children." Picking me up from the couch, Sam dragged me into the hallway, kicking me viciously as we went. "What are you going to do?" I probed.

"I'm going to kill you. Whadoo y'think!" he yelled, hitting me again. "Get down on ya knees!"

Sam put the gun to my head.

"Count to five—OUT LOUD!"

Somehow, all in a single moment, three things happened. I thought, *This is real.* A wave of sadness washed over me as I realised I would not get to experience any more of life with my family. Then a soothing wave of deep peace engulfed me because I knew where I was going.

"Five—four—three . . ."

"Run, kids. NOW!"

At the sound of Sue's voice, Sam took off, leaving me kneeling on the hallway floor.

"When I find you, I'll kill you too!" I heard him yell as he ran out into the night.

6
DESPERATE AND DIVIDED

I HAD NO IDEA WHERE MY FAMILY WAS, BUT I KNEW I HAD TO ACT *now*. Struggling to my feet with my hands still tightly tied behind my back, I stumbled back into the lounge room. The sliding door off to the side of the house was open! How did they get that bolt unlocked so quietly? I wondered. We had recently installed a bolt on that door because the original catch had never worked properly. It was tricky to manoeuvre, but someone had managed it!

Standing at the doorway, I looked out into the night. The moon had passed beyond the horizon, and it was now pitch black outside. Sam was yelling and screaming in frenzied anger as he stumbled along the driveway, waving his gun wildly. Hobbling as fast as I could, I made it out of the house, then tripped and fell painfully into the garden shrubs beside our driveway. I held my breath. I could see Sam's boots only a hand's breadth away from my face, but he didn't see me. I heard him go into the house. He began to smash whatever was in his path. I breathed a sigh of relief. *At least Sue and the kids made it out.*

I staggered to the main road at the end of our driveway, then broke into a half-running stride towards a neighbour's house. Seeing car lights suddenly ahead of me, I threw myself into the drainage ditch beside the road, panting with pain and fear. *How many guys are out there? Have they got guns? Has anyone been killed?* My emotions were through the roof.

The neighbour's gate was closed, and without the use of my hands, I didn't stand a chance of opening it. Launching myself over the top, I landed on my side on the gravel stones of their driveway. I knew which side of the house their bedroom was on, and with my sore and bloodied head, I began banging on the window.

I will never, ever forget the look on Rob and Susan's faces when they peered out at me in the dark. I must have looked like Rambo on the loose. Opening the door, they quickly ushered me inside, but by now, panic had set in. "He might be right behind me!" I whispered urgently, "Please don't turn on the lights." With shaking hands, Rob freed my wrists, then we all locked ourselves in the hall of their home while Susan, his wife, phoned the police.

My heart was racing. *Where was my family?*

At that moment, my eye was drawn to some light outside the window in the hallway. Sue had sprinted across the road to another neighbour's place, but she had come from another direction, which activated all their security lights. Sue reacted in panic and changed direction, leaping over a fence into one of their paddocks to get away. I knew the fear she felt; she thought she was being chased. Finally, we saw her stumble across the paddock towards us, and when she was safely within reach, we pulled her into the house. I nearly cried with relief. Sue was safe!

Moments later, there was a frantic banging on the front door.

It was Jason.

"I managed to get the sliding door unlocked so everyone could get out," he panted, "... then I ran to the packing shed ... and you know the stack of apple boxes ... I climbed right up high. I didn't know what to do." He was scared and out of breath.

He continued, still panting, "After a few minutes, I could hear things being smashed in the house ... I thought it was Sam ... I climbed down and ran out onto the road. I ran here, but I fell into the cattle stop and my leg got jammed."

My heart went out to my thirteen-year-old son. Throughout the whole ordeal, he had kept his head and managed an extraordinary escape. Picking up the phone once more, our neighbour called the police with an update. "Three of them are safe. We still don't know where the two girls are."

"We'll stay on the line," the police assured us. "The Armed Offenders Squad is closing in from different directions. They're checking each of your neighbours' properties and combing through the ..." The line went static for a second, and then the officer's voice came back clear. "We have your daughter. She's safe!"

"Which daughter?" we asked in confusion.

"Your eldest daughter, Michelle." Suddenly, our hearts skipped a beat. We presumed both the girls would be together. *Where was Sarah?!*

"We'll find her," the police replied. "We found Michelle at your neighbour's house. The gunman caught sight of her and chased her as she fled down the road in her pyjamas, but your brave girl outran him for five hundred metres. She's with your neighbours, Andrew and Sally. We'll bring her to you. The Armed Offenders Squad is approaching your house now. We'll keep you updated . . ."

At that point, I'm sure we all went into shock. It seemed like an eternity before the voice on the end of the phone came through with the report: "Your youngest daughter has been found! She's safe. She was curled up in her bedroom, hiding under some blankets."

Nine-year-old Sarah was still in the house?! How did Sam not see her?

Sue and I looked at each other, confused. The officer continued, "She saw the gunman chasing the others, but they were running in different directions, so she broke away and crept back to her room. She hid under the bottom bunk bed and pulled the blankets over herself. She's another brave one!"

Two and a half hours later, the Armed Offenders Squad arrived at Rob and Susan's house. These were giants of men, heavily armed in their black, war-like squad uniforms, but they spoke with calm, caring, professional voices. No doubt some of them were fathers too. "We're still looking for the intruder," they told us, "but most importantly, you're safe now." Until then, we'd tried to act brave, but when we heard those words, all five of us gave in to tears.

I can barely comprehend what went on in my mind as I faced my own death and the loss of my family. It's a terrible feeling, being so helpless and unable to protect your family and wondering when the fatal moment will come. I felt like I'd been thrust into a war and confronted with an enemy I hadn't seen coming. On top of that, my whole body was trembling with pain.

We sat in the lounge, and Susan and Rob brought everyone a cup of tea while the squad leader informed us of the next steps. "Brian, let's get you to the medical centre for some stitches. Then we'll take you all to the police station and see if we can piece together what happened."

The officers were endlessly kind and reassuring. When my head wound had been stitched and a broken rib attended to, they ushered us all into a room and began to ask questions. "Can we close the curtains?" Sue asked, looking at the large windows. We were all still on edge—and exhausted. "Of course," the officer replied kindly, "and don't worry, you're safe here."

For the next few hours, we told the police everything we knew. They were quick to string things together and soon located Sam hiding in the wardrobe of an old house in a nearby rural town.

"Sam has been arrested," the police reported to us a few hours later. "He took your car and drove to Huntly via the back roads, but rolled it when he came off the road near the river. He pulled himself out of the car and clambered down the riverbank in the dark. Apparently, he jumped into the river, thinking that he would float downstream to hide somewhere. It's remarkable that he survived. Your car was completely smashed from the roll."

It was nearly sunrise when the police dropped us back at Rob and Susan's house. We were emotionally drained, but we were safe, and most of all, we were all together.

7
EXTRA SECURITY

WAKING UP THE NEXT MORNING IN THE SAFETY OF ROB AND Susan's home, we were thankful it was all over. None of us, not even the children, had slept much for what remained of that night. As the skies lightened, we gathered around the breakfast table and began piecing our memories together into a big picture of what had occurred. We were in utter disbelief. *This sort of thing doesn't happen in New Zealand. Especially not to us.*

The clock read 6 a.m. when a loud knock at the door jolted us out of our conversation. Rob pulled the curtains open, and my heart sank. There, on the doorstep, was a group of cameramen and journalists eager to get more of the story. We gave them a few details, then closed the door.

It didn't take long for radio stations around the country to pick up the story. *A family—parents and three children—were attacked by a gunman on a rural property near Hamilton last night. The motivation for the attack is unknown.* My mum was listening to the news on her car radio when she heard the report. Meanwhile, we'd finally been able to call Sue's parents. "We'll be there in half an hour," they said. "Let's bring you back to our place for a while."

It was a comfort to be back in Sue's family home. Sue's parents, understandably, struggled to make sense of what had happened. I tried to answer their questions, but all I wanted to do was sit and stare at the wall. I felt incredibly drained. I had no words, and this was just the beginning. I didn't realise that the fallout was going to be debilitating.

Sue and her mum tried their best to keep the children busy. We were receiving constant updates and reports, as well as requests for more interviews. When television crews turned up at Sue's parents' place later that afternoon, we tried to brush off their questions.

"Did the attacker work for you?"

"What do you think his motive was?"

"What did it feel like to be tied up and unable to help your family?"

We told them we didn't want the coverage and cut the interviews short, but it was amazing how much made its way into the media. I thought of my workers and the other fruit growers in our region. I didn't want them to hear about the attack on the 5 p.m. news. It was a busy time on the orchard, and we needed to be there. But what could I do? Swept along by the demands of the day, I found myself exhausted but unable to rest.

The police advised us not to return to our home until it was properly cleaned. Our orchard manager offered to feed our dogs and manage the pickers on his own for a few days, while kind-hearted friends and neighbours went through our house, scrubbing away every trace of blood and removing any signs of damage.

None of us were prepared for the shock that would hit us when we finally returned to our property, but what could we do? We couldn't stay at Sue's parents' place forever. This was our home—but all we could see was Sam thrashing about with his gun and his knife, and all of us, petrified. For a few days, we came and went from the property during the day and slept at Sue's parents' house each night.

The following week, we made the tough decision to move back into our home. None of us felt good about it, but life had to go on. We had a business to manage, bills to pay, a garden and orchard that needed our attention, and our kids needed some sense of normality. But eleven-year-old Michelle put her foot down. The trauma of being chased by Sam was still raw. She was still on edge, tormented by the memories of what had happened that night. Reluctantly, we left her in the care of Sue's parents, and the rest of us headed back home.

Thankfully, we were not alone. When news of the attack reached my brother Phil in Christchurch, he picked up the phone. "I'm dropping everything," he said. "I'll be on the first flight up." We were thankful to have him with us in the house—especially at night when every little noise caused us to jump. We installed locks on all the bedroom and hallway doors, but in the end, we all slept together in one room just to be close to each other.

To our surprise, another man came to check on us as well. "I'm Sam's dad," he said. I could hardly believe it. Jim and his wife were shocked at what their son had done and wanted to help us in any way they could. "I'm going to put in security cameras all around your home," he insisted. Jim was a superb handyman and installed the security system and extra locks for us.

Meanwhile, the police offered us one of their Alsatian dogs. Vada had failed a small part of his police training, but as a guard dog, he was superb. Our two other dogs took to him quickly, and Vada soon became a much-loved member of our family. The police also placed us under the care of their victim support team and made sure we had access to counselling. I wasn't sure if we'd need it. *Life goes on, after all.* We were of Dutch and farming stock—pragmatic people who don't give in easily. We needed to get back to work and school. The attack was behind us now. I was sure the terrible memories would fade soon enough.

When my brother had to leave, we were all a bit sad. The children loved having him around, and he had been a great support to us in the orchard—and in the middle of the night when fear got the better of us.

Thankfully, others stepped in. Every night at midnight, our foreman drove to our place from his home twenty minutes away to walk around the property and ensure everything was fine. He continued this for several months. Another man who had worked for us for several years came and parked his old van at our front door and stayed for two weeks. And the police often dropped in to check on us. "Want a ride in the car, kids?" they'd ask. Jason and Sarah were delighted. Turning the sirens on, they cruised around the streets with the local cops, arriving back home with big smiles on their faces.

We were all relieved when, after several weeks, our brave daughter came home. "I miss being with you all, and I want to be at school and see my friends again," Michelle said. She was encouraged when she met Vada, our police-trained dog, and the newly installed locks in the house and the outdoor security lighting all helped to make her feel safe.

Finally, we were all back together again. I'd watch as the children hugged the dogs and played chase with them on the front lawn. *They're doing okay,* I thought. *We're nearly back to normal.*

We still had a way to go, but we were getting there. Or so I convinced myself.

8

AN UNEXPECTED SENTENCE

W E WERE ATTEMPTING TO DEVELOP A NORMAL LIFE—TO TRY and be happy again. The business was fast-moving and complex, and I loved it, but after hours and on the weekends, I crashed and wanted to hide from it all.

Every week, we attended counselling as a family. Sue and the kids seemed to benefit from it, but I found it a waste of time. Making the kids throw soft toys at the walls to deal with their anger seemed so pointless. "This isn't for me," I said to Sue. "You and the kids keep going if you like. I'm done with it."

But things were starting to bother me. If we came home after an evening out, I'd drive around the house, shining the car lights around the property to make sure nobody was around. I couldn't watch the news. My whole body tensed at the sight of violence.

I started taking long walks at night. Sometimes, I'd get in the car and drive aimlessly for hours on end. I didn't know it then, but the whack to my head was starting to take its toll. More and more, I found myself wanting to isolate and hide. I felt like a failure. All kinds of negative, destructive thoughts were flowing through my mind. *I failed my family. If I was a real man, I wouldn't have let this happen*. I couldn't seem to put the pieces together. The more I tried to put on a mask of normalcy, the more abnormal I was becoming. The little boy inside me was dead scared and panicking.

Meanwhile, Sue was holding us all together. She covered for me when I went off for long walks alone and never spoke badly about me to the kids. I'd sit at the dinner table in complete silence, but she kept the conversation going, masking the hurt, doing her best to make life as easy as she could for the kids.

By now, the children were back at school. They loved being with their friends and seemed to be doing well. But I was sinking. My whole personality seemed to have changed. There were times I wished I was dead. I could not even see that I had a strong family, a wonderful wife and kids who loved me to pieces. I was locked in my own abyss of hopelessness, almost attention-seeking, but it wasn't that. It was like being lost on a pitch-black night with no idea how to find my way home.

I didn't realise how much I was hurting Sue by disappearing in the car for hours or going for long walks on my own. Sadly, we had both fallen into a pattern of not talking out our problems together—how foolish that is. Sue and I had always given the impression things were under control. That had become our persona. I remember, a few years before the attack, when we mentioned to Mum that we were in financial trouble, she said to me, "I would never have guessed. You always look like you two have it all together. You're the model family." I think this was part of our downfall, not talking about the things that were happening in our lives.

I couldn't bring myself to admit I was struggling. My long nighttime walks were becoming more frequent. I didn't understand the consequences of a head injury and how the brain works, and I didn't understand depression. Friends visited to encourage us, but it seemed we couldn't be honest or explain our frustration to anyone. We didn't even understand it ourselves. All I wanted to do was isolate and hide. It was a difficult, daily struggle to cope. But for Sue and the children, it was confusing—and frightening. No one knew where I was. "It's just attention-seeking," they concluded, but that couldn't have been further from the truth—I was doing all I could just to cope on a day-to-day basis.

◆ ◆ ◆

On the morning of the trial, Sue and I sat in the courtroom like scared rabbits. Our lawyer had already told us what to expect. "We're not going for attempted murder. We need to go for a lesser charge to ensure a conviction. Between aggravated breaking and entering, wounding with intent, taking you against your will, threatening your children and unlawfully taking a motor vehicle, he's going to get at least ten years."

It had been six months since the attack, and this was the first time since then that we had come face-to-face with Sam. It was very difficult to look at the man who had turned our lives upside down on that wild night, and our emotions boiled in unexpected intensity. We listened to the back-and-forward presentations by the prosecution and defence, and for the first time in my life, I understood my father's rage. Anger and fury consumed me. I hated the man who had hurt my family. In that moment, everything in me wanted to retaliate.

Sam pleaded guilty to all four charges. He stood in the dock very subdued, unable to look at us. Towards the end of the hearing, the defence brought Sam's father, Jim, to the stand. He gave a sincere appeal on behalf of his son. He explained that they were a close family and that they were committed to caring for Sam and supporting him through and after the sentence. The judge liked the sincerity of the presentation and could see that Sam's dad was genuine. As the proceedings came to an end, the court was asked to rise. In the judge's summary statement, he acknowledged the testimony from Sam's father. We were shocked when the judge finally read out the sentence: six and a half years' imprisonment.

Six and a half years? We'd been led to expect a ten-year term at least. We wanted justice served up. Was that all Sam got for what he had done to our family? Whatever progress we had made suddenly felt meaningless. We had entered the courtroom that day grieving the loss of the peace and security we'd once had as a family. By the time we left, we were angry.

I say to all of our credit that we didn't turn on each other. Sue and I weren't angry at God, though we certainly wondered where he was. We weren't even angry at Sam himself. We were just extremely hurt by the impact of Sam's actions on our family. The anger was hard to pin down, but it was there, right below the surface.

We've never been blamers, but I didn't want us to become bitter. I wanted us to stay as sweet as we could on the inside. Sue and I knew that if the bitterness grew, it could become a monster that would eat us up. The best thing to do, we decided, was to write to Sam in prison. It was a simple letter, but every word was genuine.

As a family, Sam, we forgive you for what you've done.

9
CLUTCHING AT STRAWS

W E WERE JUST ENTERING OUR BUSY SEASON LATER THAT YEAR when we received the news: John, our dear friend, mentor and investor, had died of a heart attack. Together, we had grown the business substantially and made plans for further development, so his sudden death came as a terrible shock and sadness. This was the worst that could happen. It seemed to compound what I was already trying to understand and deal with.

But there was more to come. "Brian," a friend told me over the phone, "Just letting you know that John's brother, Andrew, is the executor of his will." Sure enough, Andrew came in with all guns blazing. "I want you off the property," he stated upfront. Sue and I looked at each other in disbelief. We loved this property, but more than that, it was part of us. We'd packed apples for other orchardists and had built great relationships with most of our staff. We'd received awards for the business. Even Robert Muldoon, our prime minister at the time, had come for a visit. Most significantly, I was the chairman of the Waikato Fruit Growers Association, and Sue was the regional secretary. These weren't roles we could just walk away from.

More importantly, we loved our jobs. My position had taken me around the country, advising politicians and business groups about the export market. I was passionate about representing our regional fruit-growing industry. I thought about the partnerships we'd created and the initiatives we'd spearheaded. As part of the National Horticultural Research Program, we had trialled an experimental variety of the Pacific Rose apple on our orchard long before it became commercially available. Growing fruit for both export and local markets made our lives busy, incredibly rewarding and satisfying.

"It's lovely having a team of people around us and working together. I don't want to lose that," I said unhappily. Sue agreed. Her fruit and vegetables supplied much of the local community. She loved watching people come and go along the path that led to our market stall.

But what broke our hearts all over again was the thought of saying goodbye to our house and gardens. Our nephews and nieces and all our children's friends loved coming to our property. We'd planted lovely gardens with beautiful specimen trees. Rose bushes stood at the end of each row of fruit trees—just like you'd see in a vineyard. The property had a tranquil feel to it, and over the years, it had become a sort of retreat for anyone who needed some time out and solitude. Every now and then, I'd wander through the garden and hear someone playing the guitar or singing quietly under the trees near the pond.

How could we possibly leave?

Sue and I sat down one evening and tried to sift through the possibilities. The original orchard we'd bought still had our names on the title. Maybe we could rebuild in the area and keep that orchard going at least. Maybe we should push back a little and see if we could at least retain managerial rights. We had invested our lives into this place, and with John, we'd made it very successful. The problem was our arrangement with John was never a legal agreement.

I regret never asking anyone to guide us during that time. I now understand why it's important not to make big decisions when emotionally drained. Andrew had worn us down from an already very low starting point. We tried negotiating for several months, but we were tired of the fight. With sadness and regret, we agreed to sell our portion of the property and move away. We resigned from our positions with the regional fruit growers' association and the local school board. When my brother Chris and his wife, Veronica, offered for us to come and stay with them on their farm in Invercargill, we gratefully accepted. The community gave us a truly heartwarming sendoff. A new life awaited us at the bottom of the South Island, but I was shattered.

Chris and Veronica received us with great love. We took on the management of a dairy farm nearby, and the kids settled quickly into their new school, regained their confidence, and seemed to feel secure even though we were in the middle of nowhere. For Sue and me, moving to rural Invercargill was a huge shock. We had no friends, we still had parts of our business to sell, and we were back milking cows again. It was difficult.

In the last twelve months, I had watched my family threatened at gunpoint, my own life had hung in the balance, we had said goodbye to everything familiar and everything we had worked for, and for some reason, we had run away to the southernmost region of

New Zealand. Perhaps we thought we were in control of what was happening, but clearly, we were not.

"You are like a bird in a cage, Brian," Sue said to me as we drove into town for church one Sunday morning.

She's right, I thought. *That's exactly how it is. I'm locked up within myself. I don't understand what's happening. I don't know who I am anymore.* I was slipping deeper into depression and didn't know what to do about it. Sue, on the other hand, seemed to be recovering and was looking at other possibilities. "I think it would be good for me to do something to get me out of the house now that the children are settled," she announced.

Just that week, Sue had been contacted by the manager of a New Zealand singer who needed a good pianist who could travel with them on concert tours for a couple of weeks, two or three times a year. This man was a close family friend of Sue's family. They'd known him for years. *Well, it will be something she can do for herself,* I thought. *It may be good for her.* If nothing else, it would be a welcome escape from watching me spiral down into an abyss of darkness and despair. I knew she loved me, but I wasn't getting any better, and it was tiring her.

◆ ◆ ◆

Twelve months later, I was still feeling very sorry for myself and not at all capable of making a wise decision, when I noticed a franchise for sale in Nelson. "I want to build our income up again," I said to Sue. "What if we bought the franchise and moved up to Nelson?"

Sue was listening. "Hmmm," she said. "It could help this negative space you're in, Brian. Maybe this could work."

I began telling her about the business. "It's retrofitting windows with double-glazing to keep homes warmer. It's like insulation, only better. I think it's a great idea! I'm pretty sure I can easily learn to install them. Mum lives there, and I know the area—it could be the new start we need."

My brother Chris advised me, "Brian, I don't think this franchise is a good investment. It's not a proven business model. I think you're being led through on a false promise. Besides, it's outside your skill set, mate."

I didn't listen. "No, I'm sure this is going to get us back on our feet again."

Full of expectation once more, we said goodbye to my brother and his family, who had lovingly enfolded us, and moved to Nelson. Sue continued touring around the country playing the piano. The children settled into yet another new school. We bought the franchise, and I sank whatever money we had into developing it. I was desperate to rebuild our finances.

10
SNEAKING SUSPICIONS

I T ONLY TOOK TWO MONTHS BEFORE THE PRESSURE BEGAN MOUNTING in my new business. With our income at practically zero, I went apologetically to a friend to ask if he could lend us some money for a little while. Sue didn't seem to mind. *She's surprisingly easy-going about this franchise,* I thought.

That night, however, I woke up sweating from a vivid dream. In the dream, I'd seen my wife in the arms of another man! I shook Sue awake. The dream was so real! "Are you having an affair, Sue?" I asked her point-blank.

"Don't be so silly," she responded. "Go back to sleep."

But something had changed. Over the next few weeks, Sue began to behave in a way that unsettled me more than the increasing evidence that the window-glazing franchise was failing. She wasn't genuinely close to me anymore. Outwardly, the change wasn't noticeable, but when you know someone intimately, you sense the changes of their heart. Six months after moving to Nelson, we were trying to hold it together for the children when, one evening out of the blue, Sue blurted out, "I'm going back to Hamilton, whether you want to come or not."

I began to reason it out. *Hamilton is her home . . . we're under so much pressure here . . . she's burnt out from trying to carry the load . . . she wants to go back to where she feels safe, and I don't blame her.*

We agreed it was a good idea. Sue would go ahead of us and stay with her parents for a few days while I packed the car with what little we now possessed and followed with the children. She would continue with her concert tours and pick up work as a specialist music teacher. We'd rent a house, get the children enrolled in school, and I would try to come up with a plan for me.

I never expected our lives could unravel even more. This time, it was Sue who began taking frequent, long walks alone. At first, I thought she was just taking time out, adjusting back again after our years of upheaval. But soon I started wondering about my dream. It had seemed *so real!* Could it be that the tour manager was having an affair with my wife? This guy was often at our home sorting out tour arrangements with Sue. *He's pretty much part of Sue's family,* I reasoned. *They've all known him for ages.*

But I couldn't put the thought out of my mind. One day, when Sue was away teaching at a school music camp, I asked one of Sue's family members if she could trust this man. Tears came to her eyes, and she replied, "I would have, but not now." She couldn't say any more. This was my cue that something was very wrong. *Surely not,* I thought. *Our marriage is for life. Sue and I are a team.*

I arranged for the children to go to Sue's parents' place after school that day, and I headed off to the beach town where the school camp was being held. This would be the moment of truth.

Sue was in the dining hall when I arrived. "You're coming with me," I insisted. She stood up and followed me down to the beach. "It's true, isn't it?" I asked, to which she responded simply, "Yes."

My heart sank as she explained that she'd fallen into a relationship with the tour manager.

"What are you going to do?" I asked.

"I'm here for the rest of the week," she replied. "I'll give you an answer when I come home."

As I drove home to Hamilton, my heart was breaking at what our life had become. *My wife, my best friend, my confidante, the mum of our children, my workmate, the woman I love, has betrayed me.* There is no describing how deeply this cut into my heart, but I had to get a grip—the kids still needed us. That night, on my knees, I prayed all of heaven would come to the rescue.

Sue returned from camp two days later. She had phoned the tour manager and told him he needed to come over to our house. It was the most awkward situation—he and I, sitting in our sparsely furnished garage, away from the kids, both anxious to hear Sue's decision. We were all uneasy.

I took the lead and asked, "What are you going to do, Sue?"

"I've decided to stay with my family," she answered. I was so relieved.

He cried.

I spoke unflinchingly, "Mate, I forgive you, but don't ever come near our home again!"

In the days that followed, we both decided I should go back to dairy farming and we would spend time rebuilding our marriage. Eighteen months had passed since the attack, and by now, I felt confident enough to answer an advertisement for the position of manager of a large dairy farm on behalf of an absentee owner. My application was returned with a 'yes'.

Within weeks of moving onto the farm, we began going to counselling. This didn't turn out as well as we'd hoped. From the outset, our counsellor pointed the finger at Sue. He made no attempt to understand the dynamics of what was going on in our lives or the root cause of the betrayal. We abandoned the counselling and battled on, but it was hard.

Many of our old friends tried to support us, but we didn't know how to be honest about our true feelings. One couple who had been very close to us over the years visited us regularly, but after a while, I became suspicious. Was my friend paying attention to Sue? There was no evidence, so I pushed the thought aside. *We're rebuilding our lives,* I told myself. *We need to choose to trust one another.*

Four years after the attack, it seemed that we were reaching some semblance of normality again. By now, Jason had finished his schooling and was working with me on the farm. This was pure joy for me—we worked together so well. The girls were happy as always. Michelle had just started high school, and our baby, Sarah, was twelve. Even better, Sue and I were about to celebrate twenty-five years of marriage.

11
AT WIT'S END

THE WEEKEND OF OUR WEDDING ANNIVERSARY, JASON WAS AWAY for a well-deserved break. Sue and the girls had helped me with the morning milking. The cows were grazing contentedly. We decided to head into town to do some shopping and have lunch. The girls enjoyed looking around the shops. "Let's buy a new lounge suite," we decided, and so we did. We wandered around awhile, then went to a lovely café for lunch. By mid-afternoon, we began heading for home. Before we knew it, it would be time for the evening milking.

When we pulled into the driveway, Sue turned around and asked Michele, "Can you step in again and help Dad with the milking?"

"Yes, of course," she replied happily.

After a quick change of clothes, we headed back out to the milking shed. Whenever my eldest daughter was milking, there was plenty of laughter. This evening was no exception. We got through the herd in good time and joked together as we traipsed back across the fields towards the house.

But our laughter quickly subsided when we found Sarah on the couch, crying. "What's wrong, darling?" I asked.

"Mum's gone!" she answered quietly. "She's written each of us a note—here." I took the note and opened it. It was short and to the point. "I don't love you anymore. Don't come after me." I crumpled the paper up and threw it away in anger. The girls were devastated.

This time, I knew deep down what was going on. I'd felt increasingly uneasy and had pressed Sue to find out if my hunch was correct. She didn't need to answer. The look on her face said it all. She was gone, and my heart was broken . . . again.

After a week, Sue made contact to say she had rented a house and had arranged for her piano to be brought over. I made myself scarce when she came around with the piano mover. It was obvious our marriage was over, but my heart couldn't handle it. It felt like I had been dealt the biggest kick in the guts a person could ever have to contend with. In every way, I'd become 'one with my mate', and now she'd been ripped away from me. The hurt was only made worse by the fact that my friend had betrayed me. Over time, it came to light that he and Sue had been in a relationship for more than a year. This man I had trusted and thought was being supportive had been messing with Sue right under my nose—and the nose of his wife!

I was furious. These were our family friends. We had gone to church together and shared meals, and he had worked for us on the farm as a contractor. His wife was devastated too. For months, she couldn't face talking to me. All the time we thought they were offering support, we were being played. *How can anyone do this to his wife and daughters . . . and to his supposed friend?* The more the thoughts raced around in my head, the more I wanted revenge. I had offers from 'big men' to go 'take him out', slash his tyres, throw eggs—all justifiable, but deep down, I knew revenge wasn't the answer. In my heart, I knew I had to let her go.

◆ ◆ ◆

After Sue left, I looked after the children, and they looked after me. I had no experience with managing a family household, so Michelle, now about fifteen, came with me to the supermarket and helped me shop. I cried up and down the aisles—still in denial—hoping Sue would come home. Michelle tried desperately to make us like a normal family. A very black-and-white thinker, she could not grasp what her mum was doing or why. For a while, she tried to reason with her, but eventually, she too had to let go and accept that her mum was involved with another man. The kids desperately wanted us together, but there was nothing I could do.

The devastating effect on the children was indescribable. I know there are some destructive situations that need to be exited, but I wanted to do everything I could to hold our family together. But it wasn't to be. Before long, Sarah, who was only twelve at the time, went to live with her mum. "It feels like I have lost my dad," she told me one day. Those were the worst words a dad could ever hear.

◆ ◆ ◆

In the meantime, I received news from the owner of the farm that it was being sold and we'd need to move. I couldn't believe it.

"I'm fed up with all this moving," I told the children.

Jason, a stalwart supporter, encouraged me, "Come on Dad, let's look for another place together." As it happened, a kindly couple we'd known when the kids were little was looking for a farm manager. What a relief! The three of us stepped straight into a new farm and a new home.

Milking the cows twice a day helped tether my mind to the present. But it wasn't enough. Mentally, I was spiralling. I understood that Sue had chosen this new relationship, but I couldn't stop blaming myself. No wonder she was gone. I had worn her out emotionally. Neither of us could handle the pressure. We were both doing our best to cope, and a new relationship looked like the answer for her.

Darkness like I had never known began to exert a grip on me. I didn't want to get out of bed and had to fight to get myself up in the mornings. The bed was the only place I felt safe. Blaming myself, feeling deep shame and embarrassment, I told myself over and over, *You've unravelled. You've failed as a man.*

The kids were something else. They just loved me. Their innocence was refreshing. They knew to love Dad while not being able to make sense of what life was dealing us. I did my best to love them back, though I was hardly capable of anything at the time. I would cry, and cry some more, day after day. Everything in me was crushed and confused. I could have filled buckets with my tears. When I went out to do the milking, I carried a towel with me to cry into—like a child with its blanky for comfort. Handkerchiefs wouldn't last five minutes at the rate I was leaking water.

After the children had gone to school one morning, I lay on the floor of the bedroom crying. I was done. I called my brother's wife in hopeless tears and blubbered almost unintelligibly down the phone, "I'm finished, Ronnie. I can't go on." She and my brother Chris had recently moved from Invercargill, and straight away, she made the two-hour journey from Tauranga, where they now lived, to come and be with me.

Someone phoned Sue; perhaps it was one of the children. When she walked into the house, she found me sobbing on the floor and my sister-in-law sitting on my bed. I reached out to Veronica with my hand and wept. I must have looked like a beggar pleading for food, "I can't do it anymore."

Sue knelt on the floor next to me and bundled me up in her arms. In my helpless state, it was decided I should be taken to the doctor. Sue drove me to our family doctor, who, after listening and prescribing some medication, advised I be taken straight to the mental health ward of our local Waikato Hospital. Sitting in the waiting room, I could hear screams, shouts and strange sounds coming from the ward. I know these facilities are a vital part of our health system, but I looked at Sue and asked, "Do you really think I belong here?"

She said nothing, so I spoke up. "Well I don't, so please take me home!"

At long last, I accepted help. The mental health team arranged regular support visits, and I started taking medication to even out my moods. Veronica phoned me every day to encourage me, although it was mostly me talking about the same things over and over, and she would just kindly listen.

"Lots of relationships come under pressure," I bemoaned. "Children die, a husband or wife dies, there's a major health crisis, someone has an affair . . . some couples work through these crises, ya'know . . . it's 'til death do we part . . . or so I thought."

"Divorce never even entered my mind. We never talked about that. Our marriage was a lifetime commitment . . . I assumed."

Veronica graciously listened to me pour out my heart, often for over an hour. Her answers were so wise. I know now that God was using Veronica to help me, but my pain was all-consuming, and I couldn't find him.

I'd get off the phone and scream out to God, "Where are you? Why are you not helping me?" *Isn't that what you do when you're in trouble? Cry out to God and he'll fix it?*

There was no quick resolution to even one of the crises we'd faced over the past decade. But for me, the pile seemed insurmountable. I'd experienced one major life-changing event after another without ever having the skills to manage them. By now, people expected me to move on—and I think I expected that too. The fallout of the attack had only been compounded by the sense of injustice that gripped me. I'd lost all our money, our family unit which had been everything to me was destroyed, and I was back to where I'd started, share-milking and living in an old farmhouse.

They say wounds take time to heal, and I have found that to be true. Slowly, I became aware of an inner sense that God was still there. His voice seemed imperceptible, but eventually, I heard his words: "Brian, I see your pain. I will comfort you."

It was time to have a conversation with God.

12

ENVELOPED BY LOVE

EACH STEP ON MY HEALING JOURNEY PEELED BACK A LAYER I HADN'T thought of before. Gradually, I began to see myself and my behaviour more clearly. I had lost many close friendships as a result of what had happened. But the issue that stopped me in my tracks was the deep betrayal by male friends.

As a child, I'd always been a bit scared of my dad, and now I realised that I saw God much the same way. Dad had been someone I feared. I was wary of him and never quite trusted him to love me and be kind.

What if God wasn't like my dad at all? What if he wasn't like any of the men who had turned on me or taken things from me or betrayed me? What if God was only kind and good and loving?

But I already had my rebuttal. "Why did you let all this happen? Why didn't you stop it all? Where were you when I needed your help?"

In that moment, I sensed his reply. "Brian, where were you when I flung the stars into space? Where were you when I created every animal, plant, bird, fish and insect? Are you aware of the beauty all around you—the stars in the sky, the galaxies beyond your view? A glorious sunset is me showing off my wonder," he seemed to be saying. "Have you noticed the variety and colour of every flower, how their beauty sings out to you with a radiant smile?"

My mind sped back to my childhood. I had been fascinated by how things worked: the path of the earth and planets around the sun, the flower petals that come in so many different colours, how bees fly, and how machines work.

Had God made me with the same beautiful and intricate care? Was he aware of my innermost workings all along?

I thought of all the pain I'd carried over the years. My dad had never really understood me, but now my heart went out to him in compassion. He was carrying his own pain. I could see it now. Even so, where was he when I needed him most?

"Can you trust me despite what you see and experience?" I heard God say.

It was a good question. Amidst all our family had been through, I felt he had let us down. "Take your time," his voice sounded reassuring. ". . . it's okay to rebuild trust slowly. I'm here with you just as I have always been. I'll never leave you or forsake you."

"And Brian . . ." I sensed his words in my spirit as if they were an afterthought, ". . . I know how it feels to be betrayed by a friend."

Something was shifting. I'd never seen God like this before. I knew God was the creator of the universe and everything around me was a gesture of his love, but I'd been taking it all for granted. In all my attempts to understand the pain and suffering I had been through, I hadn't factored in that God loved me. I still equated God's love with him 'fixing my problems'. If he sorted everything out, that meant he loved me, didn't it?

◆ ◆ ◆

I was turning all this over in my mind when calving time came around. This is an extremely busy time in the farming calendar, and I was still very tender inside. The owners of the farm were supportive towards me, "We want you to continue Brian, and we'll help wherever we can."

What relief! I'd been less than reliable for the past few months, but they believed in me. I wasn't going to be removed from the farm after all.

I began to realise how cynical I'd become. I'd stopped going to church because I felt people there had abandoned me and didn't try to understand. But my mind went to Chris and Veronica, and my son Jason, and Michelle, and the neighbours who'd taken us in on the frightful night. I thought of Sam's dad coming to install security cameras, and our orchard manager, the kindness of the police and the mental health team. I remembered Sue's arms around me as I'd wept on the bedroom floor.

So many people had shown me kindness.

I began to see that God had been showing me his love through the care of other people. I'd felt so undeserving of it all. People dropped off meals for us. Some called in just to sit with us or help wherever needed. In the midst of turmoil, God was bringing a sense of calmness to my heart. My friend Graeme and his wife were there for me every step of the way. Graeme phoned me often, just to listen and express his care for me. Sometimes, he'd turn up at 5 a.m. to help us milk the cows. Every Friday evening, Graeme and his wife would bring fish 'n chips to share with me and the kids. This couple had been close friends of mine for years. They'd been as shocked as I was at all that had happened. "God cares, Brian," Graeme would say, and then he'd pray for us. By now, Graeme had become like a father to me.

My bright, positive sister Gaylene came to stay with us for the entire three months of calving, bringing some sense of normality to our home even when I wasn't functioning well. "What do I do here, Brian?" she'd ask. I racked my brain, trying to think of the answer. This was work I had been doing regularly all my life, and now I couldn't even make a simple decision. "I have no idea," I'd finally admit. "You figure it out, and I'll help *you*." Somehow, we muddled through, the cows didn't die, the world didn't end, and by the end of calving season, we were still standing—barely! The kids helped wherever they could, rearing calves, cooking meals, giving me lots of cuddles, and just loving and accepting their broken dad. They were the most precious angels. They had so much to deal with, and they were extraordinary.

It was the love of my family and friends that gradually started a shift in me from anger and bitterness towards freedom. I didn't feel I was free yet, but I had a growing desire to be kind to the people who had hurt and betrayed me.

I kept loving Sue and praying she would return. Her leaving was so enormous it almost made the home invasion seem insignificant, and yet they were interlinked. My prayers for Sue's return were not answered, and I had to reconcile myself to that fact. I'd been brought up with firm expectations about the commitment of marriage. Now they were severely challenged, along with my perceptions of God. I want my faith to be real, not just the boring, intellectualised belief system I'd become accustomed to. I'd thought I could tick the 'good' box by going to church to please God, and then, by and large, for the rest of the time, do my own thing. I was so tired and weary of this journey. Finally, I began to see God as a loving father. He wasn't 'pleased' with me because I went to church. He didn't love me because of anything I did or didn't do. He simply loved me because I was his child.

Was it possible he could fill me with love for people once more? I knew 'panel beating' wouldn't cut it. If I was to truly forgive those who had wronged me, I needed a full restoration.

13
FACE TO FACE

I T WAS A COLD MORNING, AND I WAS OUT ON MY MORNING ROUNDS on the farm after the milking when I heard the van deliver the local newspaper. The driver leant out of his window and tossed the paper somewhere in the direction of the letterbox. I walked up the driveway, retrieved it, and wandered inside for breakfast. While Michelle was getting ready for school, I sat at the table and leafed through it. *Hmmm, nothing much . . . but hang on . . . wow!* There in the ad pages, I spotted a photo of Sam looking out at me. It was definitely him; I couldn't mistake the face. I could hardly believe it. *There he is, and I don't even feel angry,* I realised.

He was out of prison by now and was looking to set up his own business as an arborist. Right there in the newspaper was his phone number. *Extraordinary!*

I phoned him right there and then, and he answered immediately. "Sam, it's Brian!" I exclaimed warmly.

Silence.

He probably thinks I'm phoning to tell him what I think of him . . . abuse him in some way, I guess.

Breaking the silence, I began telling him a little of what had happened since that night seven years ago. I told him again that I'd forgiven him, that it was all okay. Then, to my complete surprise, I found myself saying, "Sam, would you like to come and visit me here on the farm tomorrow evening so we can talk more?"

Even more surprisingly, Sam agreed. "Can I bring my girlfriend?" he asked. I wondered if he wanted some protection in case I was out for revenge! *Quite a risk on his part,* I thought.

I told the kids that Sam was coming over the following night. The girls decided they didn't want to hang around, but Jason said, "Dad, I'll stay."

The next night, I didn't know what to expect. My heart was racing as I opened the door to Sam and his girlfriend. To my utter amazement, I felt such an affinity with this man as I shook his hand and gave him a hug. *How could this be happening?* It was like I was seeing myself from a distance as I welcomed them into our home. *This isn't how I should be reacting to the guy who turned my life upside down and inside out, trampled on me and wished me dead.*

Jason brought us each a cup of tea, and we sat down to talk. Our time together was unexpectedly pleasant. Sam was honest about the details of that night, what led to it, his time in prison, and the impact of the letter we had written him. As he spoke, I was astonished. I realised the pain, the hurt, the anger—it was all gone; I couldn't feel any of it.

◆ ◆ ◆

The healing of my hurt was a solid beginning, but I still had a lot of forgiving to do. I muddled through that year on the farm and decided for the benefit of my health, and to be fair to the couple who owned the farm, that I needed to leave full-time farming. When Michelle finished school and enrolled to train as a teacher in Tauranga, a couple of hours away, I decided to make the move too.

It was terribly hard to leave Hamilton. I had made so many friends over the many years, and it was heartbreaking to leave them all behind. Sue's family, in particular, were among my best friends. I knew this meant being disconnected from the whole family—and the closeness we'd always enjoyed. In my mind, once I moved away, that would be it. I'd be out of their lives forever. I loved and appreciated Sue's family for who they were and for all the ways they had been in my life over the years. As I said goodbye and began making my way to Tauranga, my heart was filled with an equal measure of grief and deep gratitude.

14

SOMETHING SOLID

KNOWING MY MARRIAGE WAS VERY MUCH OVER, I WANTED TO move forward positively, but it wasn't clear to me how to go about making a new start in life.

Unable to work, I sat at home for six months after arriving in Tauranga. For a few months, it was just me and Michelle, but when Sarah finished her school year in Hamilton, she came to join us. It wasn't easy for her—she had lived with Sue since she was twelve, and all her friends lived around Hamilton. Now, my only desire was to provide a stable home for our girls.

It was the first time Jason had lived away from home. My heart went out to him. Like me, he was seventeen and on his own. "Dad," he said when he phoned one evening, "This is so hard. I miss you all so much. I keep thinking about Sam and what he did to you . . . and what happened to Mum and why she left." Hearing his words, I wept from deep inside. The guilt and pain about the impact on our children resurfaced often. Sometimes the tears were uncontrollable.

To everyone else, I managed to look brave. I was in Tauranga, still pretending everything was fine, but it wasn't. I couldn't see the road ahead. I could barely think about the day ahead, let alone the future.

I hadn't made any new friends. I didn't know what to do for work. *You're not making the best of this 'new start',* I often told myself.

And then I woke one beautiful Sunday morning with an unexpected longing to be back in a church where I could settle and feel safe. "Where should I go, God?" I asked out loud, genuinely hoping he'd show me. After a good breakfast and feeling my natural optimism springing up again, I jumped into the car, and without too much thought, I drove to a nearby church I'd heard about.

I pulled into a parking space and began walking across the street towards the front entrance. I could see people gathering, laughing, saying hello to each other. *These look like friendly people,* I thought, and then . . . *Bang!* I felt like I'd walked face-first into something solid. My senses didn't comprehend it at first. The entrance to the church was still a few metres away. I tried taking another step, but the same thing happened. This time I almost fell backwards with the impact. I was stunned. It felt like I'd walked straight into a tempered glass door. You'd think I wouldn't try it again, but I did. I tried taking another step, and again I couldn't move forward. Turning around, I headed back to my car.

Somewhat disturbed but not put off, I decided to try another church the next week. Again, as I approached the door, the same thing happened. *Bang!* This time I didn't fight it. I made my way back to my car and drove straight home. *I can trust God with this,* I thought. *He'll show me where to go.*

On the third week, I decided to visit the church my brother and sister-in-law attended. I found it surprisingly easy to make it through the front door, though I must admit, I found it a bit hard to concentrate. But it was a good start, I decided. At least I was back in church.

The next time I went, Michelle and Sarah came to church with me. We sat together in a row near the middle, joining in and listening as best we could. In the middle of his message, the pastor came down from the pulpit and stood right in front of the row where we were sitting. Then the pastor began speaking in a way that made the most wonderful impact on us all.

> "God says, I don't want you to ever worry that anything like you've experienced in the past is ever going to happen again, because it's not. I'm putting a covering over it."

The pastor began to describe a picture he was seeing.

> "I see a big, white sheet, whiter than anything I've ever seen, pure and spotless, floating down from heaven. God's bringing the covering," he continued. "It's coming down and it's settling over the past. God says to you . . . I will heal, I will heal, and I will heal again."

By now, the girls were sobbing, and so was I. The pastor spoke softly:

> "God wants you to know he didn't sanction what happened. You thought he was angry with you . . . now start to see what he sees! The enemy of your soul tried to destroy you, but he did not succeed!"

The pastor paused a moment as if he was back in the vision. Then turning to us, he said:

"Yes . . . the covering is over it all now. It's settled."

In that moment, I sensed God's presence just like I'd sensed him all those years ago when Dad had taken us to hear Billy Graham speak. I knew God was so close he could feel our pain. He hadn't abandoned us after all.

The pastor went on to speak about my business.

"God says, I'll bless your business, you're not to worry about it. In his time, he'll bring it all into perspective—sequentially, precisely, step by step. God loves you intensely. He just wants you to respond, not to pull back from him. Just respond."

Although I had grown up in a Christian home, I began to understand that I'd never really responded *to* God, I'd only ever known *about* God.

What did I really believe? What did I really want?

What I wanted was to be whole again. It seemed he had placed me in this church to heal and grow. God was waiting for me to come close to him—he had been waiting all these years. I'd always been satisfied with just learning *about* him, but it was like knowing a theory. I longed for a relationship with him just as I'd longed for my relationship with Sue to be restored. But a relationship with God—what did that even mean?

Until now, I thought everything just *was*, that everyone travelled along through life being bumped and bruised, being thrown from one siderail to the other, but always striving for success and happiness.

What was becoming more important was a personal relationship with God. Like an owner's manual written for a car, God wrote the manual for my life. As the one who made me, he knew me better than I knew myself. He knew my likes, dislikes, my dreams and aspirations. *Could I genuinely know him? Could I ask him all my unanswered questions?* This was becoming real, not just theoretical. I realised I needed to grow up and stop treating God like a sugar daddy or trying to prove myself to him. As my loving father, God wanted me to be okay. He wanted me to be whole and healthy again. He wanted me to thrive once more—and he wanted an intimate, loving relationship with me!

I reflected on all those years we'd thought we could do life on our own, then come to him for help when we were in trouble. In the big picture, Sue and I had always just wanted to make lots of money, be a happy family, and help people. Perhaps I'd wanted to prove myself by being financially successful. It was what my dad had wanted too. And in some ways, that had come easily . . . perhaps too easily. Somewhere along the way, I'd stopped seeking God.

Now I began to see God in everything—the wonder of a flower, the trees and the ocean, all the animals, the beauty and diversity of people, how the whole universe runs in perfect harmony and if anything is out of harmony—if there was one slip—we wouldn't be here! My intellectual wranglings with God gave way to desire. I wanted to live! I didn't want to remain broken and sad. A glimmer of light had found its way in, and suddenly, I wanted to be healed.

15
GETTING HELP

HEALING OFTEN COMES IN FITS AND STARTS, BUT EVEN I WAS surprised to discover just how sick I really was. For many years, I'd felt mentally lost, confused. I'd come to Tauranga for a fresh start, but a year later I was still bumbling along, not getting anywhere. I couldn't tell if it was my head injury or my shattered emotions.

I tried different jobs, I tried dating, I ended up in a new relationship which only lasted six months. I even started a business. But my mind couldn't seem to settle. This is often the case with head injuries. The recovery cannot be easily measured, and each person adapts differently. For me, it was as if I had become locked in a time and place. My mind was filled with thoughts that kept going round and round in a repetitive cycle. I wanted to work, but whenever I was faced with a difficult task or a problem, I struggled to reason it through or think my way out of it.

My mind seemed to be my worst enemy. *You won't amount to anything, you're not good enough, you don't have any of the things you wanted, you don't have a nice car, home, your family is broken . . .* and so the record kept playing. *Was I to blame for what had happened that night? Had I brought all this upon myself? Could I have saved our marriage? Was God punishing me? Was life even worth living?*

Eventually, everything caught up with me. I did not have the strength to beat the depression or the restlessness. Until now, I'd resisted the offer of counselling, but I wasn't getting better on my own. Something needed to change.

The breakthrough came when my GP put aside his stethoscope after a routine physical and encouraged me to chat with him. For the next hour, I shared some of what I'd been through and what I was dealing with still. The doctor was incredibly patient. He understood the nature of the head injury I'd received. But he also helped me recognise that I was deeply depressed, which I did not want to admit.

"Brian, you need some help," he said. "Time doesn't fix everything. I'd like to refer you to a psychologist."

In my mind, it was one thing to need help on the farm or help to get out of a tough spot financially. We'd even tried to get help with our marriage. But seeing a psychologist? I hadn't even considered the idea.

Maybe the doctor picked up on my hesitation.

"You know, depression often carries a bit of a stigma, but at the root of it all, there's a lot of grief. But processing the grief can be very healing," he finished.

It was true—I felt reluctant about seeking professional help. It wasn't easy for me to admit how bad things had become. I'd been trying for years, but the GP was right: I couldn't heal myself.

It was time to let down my guard. "Book me an appointment," I said.

Seeing a psychologist was the best decision I could have possibly made. Very quickly, he helped me realise that the thoughts that had been circulating in my mind were mostly based on lies. Soon, I was able to separate out the shame and guilt from the incidents themselves. I saw how easily I became lost in my own thoughts and how that was destructive for me.

But it wasn't easy. I was thirty-eight when the attack happened, but some of my beliefs went a lot further back. I had to learn to consciously take charge of my thoughts and replace the negative self-talk with the truth.

It wasn't easy to do. The 'authentic me' had not come to the surface yet. I was living within the fragile shell of who I thought I wanted to be. I didn't realise that I had to be patient and give myself more time to heal. Through the expertise of the psychologist and the encouragement of friends, God was shaping me, working in my heart, and pouring his vast love into me, encouraging me to just *be me*.

I quickly discovered I needed to be careful about who I let in. I was still very raw, and even well-intentioned advice could have the opposite effect on me and trip me very easily. I remember once reaching out to a friend and being told, "Brian, just work harder on this, and you'll come right." Now, I became aware of the futility of that advice. I couldn't *think* myself better.

Even so, I questioned myself constantly. *Would I ever come right? Would I be normal again?* Being an optimist deep down, I knew I *could*. That optimism was exhibiting new shoots of growth, but the battle in my mind kept raging underneath. Sometimes I would just sob. It would come out of nowhere—a deep belly sob. I had to remember to tell myself: *Every tear is a tear of healing; every tear will come back as a blessing one day.*

Harnessing my thoughts took a lot of effort, but I was determined to persevere. Soon, I was able to come off my medication, which pleased me. But financially, I needed a breakthrough. I'd been without work for a year, and things were getting tight.

On the advice of my GP, I decided to apply for accident compensation. By now, I had been formally diagnosed with post-traumatic stress disorder, as well as the head injury. At first, the Accident Compensation Commission (ACC) was reluctant to accept my application. Should I appeal their decision?

My GP cautioned me, "You've got a good case, Brian, but fighting for accident compensation may add to your trauma." Now I had to figure out if it was worth it. In the end, my natural optimism won out again and I began to think about ways to progress the application. "What should I do, God?" I prayed.

The answer came one evening as I was watching television. A law professor from Victoria University in Wellington was being interviewed about a course he was teaching that was specifically about dealing with the Accident Compensation Commission. He agreed with the interviewer that the system in New Zealand was fraught with potential for abuse, but he also expressed concern about how difficult it could be to have a legitimate case approved, especially if it was complex. The professor went on to say that his third-year students would be taking on a few genuine cases to give them some real-life training. *Was this my answer?* The professor went on to explain that his students would handle the legwork and prepare the case. Then *he* would present the case to a judge. It seemed like the perfect opportunity.

When I contacted the professor, he was enthusiastic. "You have a solid case," he wrote. "I've allocated your case to one of my students." Sure enough, I was soon booked in for an evaluation with a specialist ACC assessor. *How was my mental state? What sort of damage, mental and physical, had I sustained as a result of the attack?* I was hopeful for a payout of some sort, but either way, this felt like a victory. I wasn't feeling hopeless anymore. I had taken the bull by the horns. I'd kicked the door open.

Sure enough, when the lawyer finally took my case to court, the judge ruled in my favour. What a result! The financial compensation would help me get back on my feet. But, even more significant to me was the recognition that I had indeed been through significant trauma, as had my family.

The ACC ruling helped put the past to rest. Now I could focus on my future. I was aware that I was highly sensitive and still vulnerable in many ways, but I had received the help I so desperately needed.

16
MAKING MY MARK

ARAH STAYED WITH ME FOR TWELVE MONTHS BEFORE DECIDING to move back to Hamilton to be with her friends. Michelle was becoming more and more independent, and eventually, she too decided to 'go flatting'. For me, this was the test. I'd come to grips with a lot of my past. I wasn't struggling with anger or shame any more. But there was no telling how I might respond to fresh scenarios. When I said goodbye to my daughters, it felt as if my heart was breaking all over again. Would this set me back? Could I continue to stand strong? Underneath, I was like a duck paddling frantically but still looking calm on the surface. I had welcomed change in the past, but now it was coming at me from all directions, and the ripples were disturbing the whole pond.

But the biggest jolt was yet to come. By now, I had picked up a job selling rural real estate. One day, I was doing paperwork in my office when a call came through from the reception desk. "Brian, there's a court bailiff here waiting to see you."

This was the moment I'd been dreading. I stood up from my desk and made my way to the reception area, struggling to keep my emotions in check. I felt so embarrassed that a bailiff had turned up at my work, holding the divorce papers. I wanted to tell him to go away, but there were people around and they'd already realised why he was here. *Just sign them quickly and get him out of here,* I thought. I signalled for him to sit down at an empty desk and looked at the papers in front of me.

Picking up a pen, I placed my signature at each 'x' marks-the-spot. It was time to face the heartbreaking reality that my family was now officially broken. Sadness spoke its words within me, and a tear welled up. I passed the signed papers to the bailiff, and he put a hand on my shoulder in a gesture of kindness. He must have understood.

I walked back to my desk, my heart a jumble of emotions . . . but my mind was at peace. It was a watershed moment for me. The feelings were real, but they weren't leading me back to the dark places of the past. My inner strength had returned. There were no voices of condemnation or fear. I was sad as sad could be, but in my mind and heart, all was well.

Four years had passed since the girls had moved out. Was I stuck in some sort of holding pattern? Up to this point, I'd only been working to make a living. Now I thought there was room for more.

I had spotted a senior management role advertised by a large farming company with ownership of a hundred and fifty large farms throughout the country. These were dairy, beef, sheep or deer farms. I thought about the idea of a senior management position. I knew that I enjoyed leading people and walking alongside them. *If I could be back in the farming industry, this could be ideal,* I thought.

On paper, I wasn't qualified for the position. All the same, I made a tongue-in-cheek application.

Unbelievably, I was invited to an interview with the company executives and was offered not one but a choice of two jobs—one based in the Waikato region and one in the Manawatu, a region further down the country from Tauranga. I was blown away. *Which one should I take?*

By now, I'd learned the value of seeking good advice. Picking up the phone, I called Graeme, the friend who had been like a dad to me since our family had broken apart. Without a moment's hesitation, he replied, "C'mon Brian, let's go down to the Manawatu and look at them both. I'll come with you."

We drove to Manawatu to get a feel for the farming industry there, then headed back north to the Waikato where I'd started my farming career. Even before the end of the trip, we both knew the Manawatu job was the one, and I accepted the role.

I later found out that there were thirty-five applicants for these two positions, and many of them were candidates with experience from within the company. Now I had something to look forward to, plus the backing of a solid expression of trust in my ability. But this was a big move. My children would be five hours away from my new location. The responsibility was not just for one farm but many. Some of my friends were concerned about what I was taking on, but I'd had the boost my confidence needed. I was ready to make the move.

My first concern was to find a place to live. I wanted to be within driving distance of the head office in the capital, Wellington, and have easy access to the two main highways so that I could cover the lower half of the North Island. I was about to start looking when I recalled that during my job interview, one of the guys had mentioned that he and his wife often holidayed at a little place called Foxton Beach. He'd described the broad, sandy beach, the birdlife, the great fishing, and some of the local characters they'd met there. "A great place to get away and reconnect," he'd said.

Get away. Reconnect. Those words jumped out at me. Despite the demanding new role, I wanted to give myself space to heal.

"God, would you show me the house you have for me there?" I asked as I scrolled through the properties for sale.

Instantly, I spotted an ideal-looking house facing right over the beach. *Surely that was too easy,* I thought. *I'd better go look.* Off I headed the next day on the five-hour drive to Foxton Beach. I felt nervous and slightly excited—like a young man leaving home for the first time, wondering what his new independence would bring. I had arranged for a real estate agent to show me around all the houses for sale, and we spent the day going from one to another. Right at the end, we pulled up in front of the last house on his list. Sure enough, it was the house I'd already seen online, and in reality, it looked just as perfect.

The older couple who owned the property bent over backwards to help me. I needed to relocate soon, and they were more than obliging. We signed the papers and set the settlement date for six weeks' time. In the meantime, the company had offered to put me up in a local motel.

◆ ◆ ◆

On the day I was to take possession of the property, I checked out of the motel and walked up the road to my new home. There, to the right of the front door, was a handmade, driftwood-style bench, and on it lay a big, beautiful bunch of flowers to welcome me. I was in awe of what God had done in bringing me here.

The wind in my face and the smell of the ocean cleared my mind. I felt free. The sobs that had for years risen unexpectedly within me subsided. I knew I was getting so much better in myself. I purchased a beach buggy so I could drive along the sand and go on fishing expeditions. I spent some time with friendly neighbours, just talking, gardening or fishing. They would dig up plants from their own gardens and bring them over to help me create mine. At long last, I had begun to enjoy my simple, little piece of the world.

◆ ◆ ◆

The unofficial policy in my new company was to throw a new employee into the deep end and see if they'd sink or swim. I have to admit, there were times I thought the job I'd taken on was too big for me. This was nothing like being a local farmer. My new role involved interacting with head office staff, executives and the chief executive officer of a large, multi-million-dollar company. Nevertheless, I thrived on the challenge. I was learning new things, meeting new people, and mostly, dealing with the responsibility—which was significant. I was being stretched, but I was growing in so many ways. This job was just the tonic that I needed.

My second year, however, was tough. Part of my job involved setting and managing farm budgets, and that year, costs seemed to mushroom out of nowhere. Mainly, it was the amount of cow-feed, but it pushed us one million over our budget.

I was in my office one day when the CEO called. I knew this conversation was coming.

"How are you, Brian?" he asked.

I replied. "I'm okay, but my seat is quite hot at the moment."

I'll never forget the wise gentleman that he was. All he said was, "That's all I need to hear, Brian. I know it won't happen again," and I can say it never did. Admittedly, I had a few sleepless nights wondering if the axe would finally fall. It wasn't easy—I had to transition some staff out, find forty new staff, buy milking cows, machinery and whatever was required to run several large dairy farms—all with a very tight handle on the purse strings.

I began to see that with God, all things are possible. All those years running our own business, which had been incredibly tough at times, had not been wasted. My experiences had developed in me a huge amount of empathy for people, which gave me a unique style of leadership: People first—care for them, pay them well, take them along on the journey of setting goals—and the rest takes care of itself. There was no need to strive or be anxious.

Over the years, my division of the company became a tremendous success, winning several awards for farming excellence. I was so proud of the team. I knew it was blessed by God, and I remembered how he'd reassured me with his words, "I'll bless your business, don't worry about it." Some of the things we were achieving confounded people in the industry. We were innovative and making our mark in the dairy industry. This company was a place where people really enjoyed working.

As the company reached new heights, so did my job. I was not qualified, but I felt divinely equipped. Being privileged to travel all over the country, I met many good people. My skills were continually stretched, and I was able to take part in management courses and training in New Zealand and Australia. Most importantly, I was back to myself, though quite a different version of me. My confidence and self-worth were restored.

I'm a grandfather now and have grandkids of the age our kids were at the time of the attack; I cannot imagine them going through what we did. It seems like a terrible dream—somehow not real but nonetheless true. For years, I had been hugely disappointed in how my life had turned out, but learning to simply trust God to take care of me was a game-changer. He knew me before I was born. He knew what was in me and what I was capable of. I'd tried to make sense of my life for years, but I'd only complicated things. *God's ways of doing things are so simple,* I finally realised.

EPILOGUE

I BREATHED OUT WITH A SATISFIED SIGH AS I SAT ON THE HOMEMADE driftwood bench in front of my house. It had been a good week at work. Setting my cup down beside me, a thought wandered its way quietly into my awareness. I remembered the letter Sue and I had written to Sam while he was in prison. "As a family, we forgive you for what you did," we had stated.

Back then, I'd written the letter because it seemed the best way to put an end to the bitterness and hatred that was growing in my heart. But something different was happening now. Sitting in front of my little house at Foxton Beach, I grasped for the first time that the simple fact I'd written those words was enough. The job of forgiveness was already 'done.'

Finally, the penny was dropping. Even though we'd written the letter, I'd still felt anger and hurt for a long time. I'd been tormented by my thoughts: *No, Brian, you haven't forgiven Sam. If you've forgiven him, why do you still have all these negative feelings?* I realised I didn't need to carry any guilt. The written words were all the evidence that was needed.

Forgiveness is an action, not a feeling. Writing the words had been the key.

I thought back to when I'd invited Sam and his girlfriend to visit our home that evening. I remembered opening the door to him and being stunned that I harboured no feelings of hate, no desire for payback, no resentment.

I wouldn't mind seeing him again, I thought.

Many years later, I was driving back from a visit to my daughter when a strong impression came to me: *I should text Sam's parents and see if I could drop in on my way home.* I thought about how often they'd kept in touch to see how I was and let me know they were praying for me. I'd drawn a lot of comfort from that. They returned my text, "Sure, Brian. We're home."

I had met up with Sam's parents occasionally over the last several years, but this time, something seemed different. As we chatted easily among ourselves, I felt a gentle nudge to ask, "Would it be okay if I tell you more about what happened that night?"

They agreed.

I found myself speaking to them about the attack, checking in as we went along to make sure they were still okay hearing it. *Yes, they wanted me to continue.* When our conversation began to wind down, Sam's dad left the room for a few minutes and returned with his ukulele. Sitting down, he began to sing, and then we quietly prayed together.

Driving home that night, I experienced an overwhelming sense of love for Sam that remained with me for several days.

Was I finally free from the imprisonment of the grudge? It felt like it.

I decided to contact Sam once again. Picking up the phone, we chatted awhile and then I asked, "Would you like to catch up next week if I drove up to your place, Sam?"

With no apparent enthusiasm, he agreed, "Yup, see you then."

The next week, Sam opened his front door to me. We spent an entire afternoon talking honestly.

"I am so ashamed, man," he wept. "I feel so unworthy, so guilty. I think about the details every day."

I reached out a hand to his shoulder to reassure him that I'd forgiven everything. "What was happening in your life back then?" I asked him.

Sam explained the grudge he'd held against me and how he'd planned to kill me. He answered all my questions. He said that when he gave me his address, he knew I could have sent a hitman, and he'd resigned himself to that. If that was the case, Sam had decided he deserved it.

In that moment, I looked at Sam and knew I loved him as a brother.

How do you explain such love? How can two men, both so lost in lies and self-condemnation, finally be set free?

Sam's story is not mine to share. It's powerful, but a very different one from mine. I know that had I not forgiven Sam, he would not have been free to receive the healing that he has. Today, he is not tied to me because of unforgiveness, and I am not tied to him.

Sam has a family of his own now, and he is an excellent dad. Twenty years on, he is still astonished that we have arrived at this place where we can be friends. It makes no logical sense to many people, but this is the power of forgiveness.

Recently, I received a notification on my phone. It was Sam. "Brian, mate, I count you amongst my closest friends." What a privilege.

AUTHOR'S NOTE

I HAD GIVEN UP ALL HOPE. I FELT THAT I HAD FAILED IN SO MANY ways, that I wasn't loved, and *what was the point of being here?* I deeply understand those emotions—and the incredibly deep pain people can feel. But now, on the other side, I see a future full of hope and sunny days, as you can. I still have bad days, just like you, but even on the bad days, I am anchored to hope and peace. My sole purpose in sharing this story is to demonstrate there is filled-to-the-brim hope, a hope against all odds! In our world today, it is easy to turn on one another or lose hope in times of difficulty. But there is another response. Let's be those who encourage each other, help each other, and focus on what the future might hold.

There are some basic, but not always easy, steps we can take towards hope. Here are four principles that have helped me become a more authentic, honest, genuine, and refined but imperfect version of myself, which I trust will, in a very small way, help you.

Choose to Forgive

Unforgiveness sometimes seems like a large and difficult hurdle to overcome. It arrives unannounced, usually from deep hurt, and lurks at our front door like a robber wanting to steal our most valuable possessions. We all, at times, struggle with offence, hurt, anger and grudges. People can be mean, often unintentionally, but it still hurts, and some offence occurs, leading to a grudge before we even realise that something has planted its tentacles into our hearts. Like a canker in a sick tree, unforgiveness slowly permeates our entire being, often with devastating impacts on our health, both mentally and physically, until we become a prisoner in a cell that we do not know how to wrestle free from. Only forgiveness can set us free.

Please use this practical step to aid you in breaking free: *Write down who you desire to forgive. Tuck the piece of paper or memo away somewhere and ignore all the negative emotions as best you can. When you feel guilty or the memory resurfaces, tell yourself, "No, I have forgiven that person. It's in writing." That is your reference point. You have done your part to be free. Now allow the process to do its work. Through God, you can do it. It may take months or years for the negative feelings to subside, but they will.*

Choose to Trust God

God is my Dad, my friend. I can talk to him about anything and everything at any time. The same is true for you. He is interested in the most minute details of your life and cares deeply for you. Even though we may not understand the 'whys', he welcomes our questions. He is not offended by our honesty. My prayers have not always been answered in ways I wanted or expected—nonetheless, he has walked beside me, weaving good things into my life, holding me, and whispering, "C'mon, I have you!"

Yes, he loves you beyond words and wholeheartedly desires a relationship with all of us despite our mistakes. No one is so far gone that his love cannot reach. Certainly, there will always be mystery this side of heaven. People have genuine feelings and free will. But no matter what storms are raging around us, we are clothed with purpose. We can have a strong inner peace, free from anxiety and worry because God cares. That excites me! The creator of all things is interested in 'just me' and the smallest details of my life. His abundant and never-ending love is for us in every situation. Whether on the mountain tops or in the deep valleys, he is right there, closer than a close friend would be. That's his promise.

I am very much still learning and growing, but I have discovered true gems in God's plans for my life. There is pure joy in seeing his beauty in people and in creation all around us. Choosing to trust in God brings a wonderful inner peace that is not available any other way.

Guard Your Marriage

I realise this topic can raise many emotions, and it is also far bigger than what I propose to cover. However, before you consider leaving your marriage, take a long pause and consider—except in cases of abuse, which should not be tolerated.

Marriage is the most beautiful institution. It has significant benefits for our well-being and provides safety for children. It can also bring the greatest joy, despite what you may be dealing with right now. However, it requires selflessly laying down our lives for others. Please stay away from affairs—they are completely selfish, extremely destructive to both adults and children, and the love you shared at the beginning of your marriage can be rekindled if the correct help is sought. Exercise commitment and integrity, be an example, and talk through whatever comes along. It's not the size of your problems, it's the size of your commitment that counts.

With fifty percent of marriages failing, our society is bearing the consequences of broken families. Adults often have no understanding of the lifelong damage that an affair or divorce inflicts on their precious children. It really does 'blow up their planet'. The levels of emotional distress and trauma our children experience are often catastrophic, especially when unmitigated by the maturity of adult understanding. They really do deserve better. Please do what it takes to put others ahead of your own desires. It may require some hard work, but you will be rewarded in the most joyful ways, I promise. Very rarely does chasing our feelings and fantasies bring lasting happiness.

Reach Out For Help

If depression, anxiousness, stress or mental trauma has descended upon you like a dark hovering cloud, so close it has enveloped you, and if it will not leave because of life's circumstances, I encourage you—your future does not need to be defined by this. You don't need to pull back, withdraw, and draw the curtains around your life. Acknowledge to a friend you trust that you are in pain, that you are struggling and need help. Do some self-care activities. Prioritise good sleep, a good diet and plenty of water, and address any underlying psychological or physical problems that need attending to. Again, forgive people who have hurt or grieved you and try to allow the healing of broken relationships.

You may need help to address the stress in your life. Remember, people sincerely care, and professionals are very good and will help you regain your equilibrium, perspective, balance and joy in life once again. My mistake was not reaching out until I had no choice, and much time had been wasted. Sometimes life throws us such heavy curve balls, and we do not always have the tools, the emotional strength or the fortitude to work our way through this journey alone.

It's not weakness to reach out for help—it really isn't. You have a robber at the door of your life, wanting to take you down, and he requires fending off. It does, however, take courage, which you have. So please, be *brave*, look this in the eye, and say, "No! Enough is enough. I am opening the windows of my life, breathing in new air, seeing the beauty that surrounds me, and walking boldly into my wonderful and exciting future, completely free and whole!"

Let nothing hold you back or defeat you. Your family and your friends are cheering you on and need you. I am cheering you on too, because you have a special place in this world, and without you, it isn't complete.

ACKNOWLEDGEMENTS

My children, Jason, Michelle and Sarah. What a privilege to have each of you in my life. Your love, sincerity, genuineness and kindness make me so proud of you. Despite it all, you are the most wonderful adults and parents to your own children. I am daily inspired by you, which gives me deep joy, and I count it a genuine privilege to be your dad. I love you beyond words.

Chris and Veronica. You have given so much to help me at crucial times. You abandoned a holiday to come to us, talked for countless hours, encouraged me and held me up. I could keep walking because of your countless small acts of kindness. You provided a place of refuge when I needed it and treated my children as your own. Words will never be able to express my gratitude, love and appreciation for all you have done.

My four siblings. We have walked through life together and stayed true to each other. You have always been there, ready to help in so many ways. Your selflessness in dropping everything to come to help our family without complaint, as well as your love for the children and patience in walking beside us as we healed, will always be remembered. I love you all.

Mum. You have walked a very challenging journey at times throughout your life, but you have always given your best for your family. Raising five children is a huge job in and of itself and we each thank you, love you, and acknowledge all you have given.

Phil Pigneri. You encouraged me to write this story. Thank you for your love, support and wise counsel. You are one of the kindest, most gentle and most sincere men I know. I pray this book helps and touches readers and brings freedom to many lives, just as you anticipated—a desire driven by your love to see people succeed in life.

Pastor David Dishroon. Your wisdom and love travel with me every day. You completely give of yourself in countless ways. Your wise words over the years and your care and love encouraged hope, making me feel I was the only one. Sincere thanks.

Graeme Fullerton and Russell Brown. You were my rocks, my second and third dads. Despite your own great losses, you remained the happiest and kindest of men. Thank you for being there whenever I needed a helping hand, sound advice, or a shoulder to cry on. I miss you both.

Anya McKee, publisher extraordinaire, thank you so much to you and all your team at Torn Curtain Publishing for your effort in helping bring this project together with kindness and compassion. You believed in this story and without you, this book would not have happened.

Friends. There are just too many of you to acknowledge by name, many lifelong friends. Each of you is an integral part of my life and highly valued. Though friendships come in and out of our lives like the tide, each one of you has made an indelible contribution and is incredibly precious. You make the world a better place and are a true gift to me. Thank you!

ABOUT BRIAN

Today, I find abundant pleasure in the simple little experiences life offers us that I once took for granted. Residing in the beautiful Bay of Plenty, the kiwifruit capital of New Zealand, on a small rural property, gives me opportunity to spend time out in the fresh air, sometimes just leaning on the fence, taking in the surroundings, the glistening green grass, the cattle chewing, and looking at me and thinking, *Wow!* Some days, I'll stroll on one of our stunning beaches or take a walk in the forest, admiring the view or a breathtaking sunset bringing a close to the day. Sometimes it's a drive in the country or coffee at a café, 'chewing the fat' with one friend or another and laughing freely. I enjoy reading, sport, and being connected to the agriculture sector, enabling me to help farmers maximise their on-farm performance.

I am beyond blessed to have family nearby who are all great company. I take great joy in being with my children and eight grandchildren, indulging in the love that we share with an overwhelmed and truly thankful heart.

What surprises me most is the indescribably deep joy, peace and contentment that underscores my everyday, despite what might be happening. To me, that is what counts as a successful life well-lived. It is opposite to how I once was, always chasing something to satisfy my inner longing for those qualities. I am grateful for the, at times, debilitating experiences of my life, for I have been transformed in so many positive ways. I am grateful simply for the gift of this life and for the deep understanding and empathy it has given me for the hurting, so I can hopefully, in a small way, help others to see life as I do.

Most of all, I give all thanks to my heavenly Father, for without him walking beside me, I would not have made it to the point where everything in life now makes complete sense. I have enjoyed a front-row seat as he turned even the most dire of circumstances into victories. He is more real to me than anything else, and today, I want for nothing. I am privileged and blessed beyond measure.

brian@maxnet.co.nz

 **@attackedbook**

For God so loved the world that he gave his one and only Son, that whoever believes in him shall not perish but have eternal life. For God did not send his Son into the world to condemn the world, but to save the world through him.

John 3:16-17

www.ingramcontent.com/pod-product-compliance
Lightning Source LLC
Chambersburg PA
CBHW021652120626
46545CB00002B/821

9781991299697